Seer's Portal:

A Review of Methods and Practices Prescribed by the New Seers

Dean Hunter

ISBN-13: 978-0-578-49919-2

To navigators of the unknown

Table of Contents

... our normal waking consciousness, rational consciousness as we call it, is but one special type of consciousness, whilst all about it, parted from it by the filmiest of screens, there lie potential forms of consciousness entirely different. We may go through life without suspecting their existence; but apply the requisite stimulus, and at a touch they are there in all their completeness, definite types of mentality which probably somewhere have their field of application and adaptation. No account of the universe in its totality can be final which leaves these other forms of consciousness quite disregarded.

- William James, *Varieties of Religious Experience*

FORWARD

****

The two-word title of this book wholly characterizes the content within. The word *Seer* represents a class of human beings that have the capacity to *see* beneath the social and material veneer that ordinarily obscures the energetic essence of everything. More often than not, such beings acquire their extraordinary ability through arduous training, unrelenting dedication and secretive practices. By all indications, the essential practices and methods described herein were passed down to Carlos Castaneda, and his cohorts, from the seers of ancient Mexico through countless generations that refined and perfected the various techniques. An informed reader will see many parallels between these methods and other spiritual/religious/mystical practices. However, the shamanic practices prescribed by Castaneda exhibit unique qualities such as; simplicity and directness, an elegant efficiency in their power to create change, and an integrated coherence in their complementary support of each other.

The word *Portal* is used for both its literal and metaphorical meaning as a door, a gate, and an entrance into "something more than, and above all something different from, the carefully selected utilitarian material which our narrowed, individual minds regard as a complete, or at least sufficient, picture of reality" (1 p. 12). The practices and methods discussed in this review can be described as: an opportunity for the dedicated practitioner to enter into new aspects of being by enhancing their perception and expanding their awareness; or a doorway to perceptions beyond ordinary reality; or an entrance into other worlds.

According to Castaneda, humans are composed of two parts; the physical body and the energy body, and the shamanic practices he advocated are primarily aimed at developing the energetic component of humans, since this is the part that can survive beyond bodily death. The idea that a soul, or some component of humans, can survive beyond death is shared by many of the world's major religions. Even science leaves room for such a possibility - acknowledging that the human body does indeed return to the dust of the earth, but energy can never be destroyed. Ultimately, the seers' practices offer a pragmatic opportunity for cognition to be maintained beyond bodily death.

References

1. **Huxley, Aldous.** *The Doors of Perception.* London, UK : Penguin Random House/ Vintage Classics Publishers, 2004.

INTRODUCTION

****

In 1961, as an anthropology student attending UCLA, Carlos Castaneda began to write about his thirteen-year apprenticeship with a Yaqui Indian shaman named don Juan Matus. Over a period of nearly forty years, Castaneda authored a total of twelve books describing his encounters with the enigmatic teacher and his cohorts. While the terms sorcery and sorcerer were used extensively in his earlier books, Castaneda (1 p. vii) (2 p. ix) later explained the terminology was not really accurate, and in his subsequent books Castaneda shifted to the terms "shaman" and "seer" in place of sorcerer. However, he ultimately made a crucial distinction, explaining that the *ancient sorcerers* were in search of power and consumed by self-importance, while the *new seers* were in search of freedom of perception, and worked tirelessly to dethrone self-importance.

Castaneda was initially showered with praise for his stupendous accomplishments, but as the years passed, new volumes were released and a whirlwind of speculation was fueled by the public's curiosity and growing doubt, as well as the man's reclusive lifestyle. Long before his death in 1998, his life's work became shrouded in controversy. Much of the negative commentary surrounding his work stemmed from four primary allegations; 1) Castaneda never provided any concrete proof to substantiate his claims, such as pictures, recordings or public demonstrations, 2) his ideas were suspiciously similar to other beliefs, philosophies and previously published works, suggesting plagiarism or hoax, 3) inconsistencies and contradictions were identified in his work, and 4) he apparently conducted his personal life in a manner contradictory to his writings and public pronouncements. Unfortunately, these allegations caused many to consider his work fraudulent and to dismiss it without due consideration.

However, such allegations neglect the essence of his work by failing to examine the various methods and practices that he described and promoted. Essentially, the subject matter of Castaneda's books can be grouped into three general categories; 1*) the philosophy of the Shamans of ancient Mexico*, 2) *the shamanic practices and methods taught to Castaneda by his teachers*, and 3) *Castaneda's personal experiences during his exposure to the shamanic methods and philosophy*. The first category, *the philosophy of the Shamans of ancient Mexico* described by Castaneda, does provide various explanations and rationales for the practices, but that philosophy could only be validated by those ancient shamans. The items in the third category, *Castaneda's personal experiences*, are beyond validation because they are purely subjective reports under unique circumstances. Although, Castaneda (3 p. 120) maintains that personal validation is possible through sustained practice. Fortunately, the second category, *the shamanic practices and their effects* can be probed for scientific validation. Indeed, the practices and methods are the only testable component of the three categories. Consequently, the validity of Castaneda's work should depend on the effects of the practices he described, taking into consideration the full scope of his work; including the twelve volumes he authored, as well as the relevant books authored by his associates, Taisha Abelar and Florinda Donner.

In the figurative language of Thomas Hennell (4 p. 4), one could say that Castaneda's books are a record of his journey to the "secret edges of the mountain"; a documented attempt to "bring home strange flowers - which are the very accusations of trespasses".

> The great experience is disowned by religion, by science, by policy. Truth must slowly find her form, and by gradual testimony. We may not choose what we shall find, nor where it shall be found. There is a French proverb: Where the goat is tethered, there it must browse. There are places where goats may wander but where children must not venture, nor go to touch them. And I have thought that if it were not so, the simple, making their way to secret edges of the mountain, might there find no goat, but Pan himself, whose piping so changes and charms all spirits that hear it.
>
> Or if not so, at least some may bring home strange flowers - which are the very accusations of trespasses. That enchanting beauty which they had is soon fled from them, and it is idle to expect those who stayed at home to believe in their beauty, or that they were once a true revelation, and promised a new, sublime world.
>
> "No," say the elders, "they are delusive; those plants are poisonous."
>
> One who has enjoyed these, may not bring them back to life, he can only say where he found them, and what they seemed like when they were fresh.

In metaphorical terms, we believe this review will show that the methods and practices, presented by Castaneda, can lead the practitioner on a journey to Hennell's "secret edges of the mountain". Like a sailor preparing to venture into the unknown, the methods and practices begin by preparing the practitioner for the journey ahead, through the accumulation of tools and skills necessary to venture into new territory. The essential tools and skills are acquired by *enhancing perceptual abilities,* which consequently draw hidden resources to the surface. Next, of course, every journey requires the traveler to depart from their present location. In the words of André Gide, "One doesn't discover new lands without consenting to lose sight, for a very long time, of the shore". So, in preparing to leave behind the ordinary world of everyday, the shamanic practices and methods enable the practitioner to detach from the everyday world and dissolve the ties that bind them by *freeing awareness from the attachments, patterns and routines of ordinary daily awareness*. And finally, *by activating new possibilities for perception that lie beyond the boundaries of ordinary daily awareness*, the doors of perception are flung open, and a path to "secret edges of the mountain" comes into view.

In practical terms, this review seeks to explore the methods and practices presented by Castaneda, and address the hypothesis that the shamanic methods provide a means for practitioners to enhance perception and expand their awareness beyond the confines of *ordinary daily awareness*. Based on the descriptions of various practices provided by Castaneda and his companions, this essay attempts to explain and validate the effects of the shamanic practices, by surveying the available scientific literature for supporting evidence. The significance of these shamanic methods is their ability to be efficient and effective tools for enhancing perception and expanding awareness. Therefore, according to our hypothesis, the practices advocated by Castaneda enhance perception and expand awareness; 1) by improving various cognitive processes associated with perception through training; 2) by reducing attachments to the patterns and routines of *ordinary daily awareness*; and 3) by activating new possibilities for perception that lie beyond the boundaries of *ordinary daily awareness*.

In summary, this review examines claims made by Castaneda and his associates, regarding the practices he advocated, and presents a collection of scientific research, and other relevant material, which support Castaneda's claims that the practices and methods he prescribed are conducive to enhancing perception and expanding personal awareness. The supporting scientific evidence presented here is by no means exhaustive, but representative of peer reviewed research that supports our thesis. Additional information can be found in the bibliographies of the references cited throughout.

References

1. **Castaneda, Carlos.** *The Art of Dreaming.* New York, NY, USA : First HarperPerennial / HarperCollins Publishers, 1994.

2. —. *The Power of Silence: Further Lessons of don Juan.* New York, NY, USA : Washington Square Press / Simon & Schuster Inc., 1987.

3. —. *Magical Passes: The Practical Wisdom of the Shamans of Ancient Mexico.* New York, NY, USA : HarperCollins Publishers, Inc., 1998.

4. **Hennel, Thomas.** *The Witnesses.* New Hyde Park, NY, USA : University Books, 1967.

CHAPTER 1

Perception

****

We necessarily begin with a discussion of perception and awareness, since these are central to our hypothesis. It is essential to establish a detailed definition of perception and to identify its fundamental processes because the methods and practices advocated by Castaneda are purported to enhance perception and thereby expand awareness into an area of greater possibilities. Briefly, we define perception as *the interpretation of the energy at large*, and awareness as *the subjective ability to experience or feel*. Perception is then, the avenue through which awareness experiences the energy at large. Therefore, when the ability to *interpret the energy at large* is enhanced, the *scope of experience* is expanded. And while perception is typically regarded as a psychological process, it also has physical correlates, particularly neural correlates. A detailed examination of perception is required, since our literature search will specifically seek to identify any effects the shamanic practices may contribute to enhancing perception.

Awareness, or consciousness as it is sometimes called, is the foundation of Castaneda's work, giving purpose to the practices he advocated and forming the essence of the philosophical rationales he described. The clearly stated goal of the methods and practices promoted by Castaneda (1 p. 27) and his associates, Abelar (2 p. xii) (2 p. xiii) and Donner (3 p. i), is **to enhance and expand the scope of individual perception and awareness**.

Awareness is a unique phenomenon that is not well understood by the scientific community, but there are measurable characteristics, such as physical correlates of awareness and psychological parameters, as well as objective and subjective methods for examining its characteristics. For example, awareness is presently being *objectively* explored using neuroimaging techniques such as EEG, fMRI and PET to examine the physical operation of the brain in order to map neural correlates of consciousness (4) (5) (6). Other researchers are using *subjective* reporting to explore the "inner experience" of consciousness by probing aspects of awareness such as dreaming and the development of consciousness (7)

(8). In addition, psychological parameters of awareness are often assessed using cognitive tests to evaluate functions such as attention and memory (9) (10).

Castaneda affirmed both physical and psychological aspects of awareness. Specifically, Castaneda (11 p. 139) (12 p. 220) acknowledged a physical connection between the body and awareness, citing various physical conditions that alter perception, including: fever, hunger and psychedelic drugs. Indeed, Castaneda's first two books contain detailed information about his perceptual experiences with the plants he identified as Datura Inoxia, Psilocybe Mexicana and Lophophora Williamsii. These plants are known to possess chemical reactants, which are classified as psychedelic drugs because they produce "thought, mood and perceptual changes otherwise rarely experienced except in dreams, contemplative and religious exaltation, flashes of vivid involuntary memory, and acute psychoses." (13 p. 9).

There is ample scientific evidence to implicate the physical body, and specifically the nervous system, as a key participant in perception. For example, numerous documented cases exist where patients suffering from traumatic brain injury, dysfunction or lesions of the brain, experience altered perceptions such as memory loss, psychoses, hallucinations and the inability to recognize familiar objects. Therefore, it is consistent that the belladonna alkaloids found in Datura Inoxia are classified as "anticholinergic because they block the action of acetylcholine, a nerve transmitter substance that … plays an important role in the chemistry of the brain." (13 p. 30). Furthermore, the neurotransmitter serotonin is an indole, like the psycho-active chemicals found in Psilocybe Mexicana, and the neurotransmitters dopamine and norepinephrine are phenylalkylamines like mescaline (13 p. 240), implicating the chemistry of neurotransmitters as the mechanism for the psychedelic effects and perceptual alterations caused by these plants. Historical evidence (14) indicates that shaman regard the intimate connection between perception and the physical body as a strategic opportunity to employ the physical body, in various ways, to broaden the scope of awareness beyond the limits of ordinary perception. Clearly, psychedelic drugs have the power to disrupt *ordinary perception*, potentially exposing awareness to new possibilities.

Castaneda also acknowledged the psychological aspects of awareness, including experience, memory, cognition and perception. In this respect, all of Castaneda's books remained true to the central themes of knowledge, perception and awareness; beginning with the task of becoming "a man of knowledge", and ending with his lucid discussions of awareness, including its fundamental and mysterious nature. Indeed, Castaneda (15 p. xii) employed a definition of *cognition* that is consistent with modern scientific descriptions.

> By cognition, it is meant the processes responsible for the awareness of everyday life, processes which include memory, experience, perception, and the expert use of any given syntax.

Cognitive psychologists use the term *cognition* in reference to processes, such as experience, learning, memory and perception, that are essential to developing strategies and behaviors for coping with the environment. Similarly, Neisser (16 p. 4), a pioneer in cognitive psychology, provides the following definition for cognition:

> ... the term "cognition" refers to all processes by which the sensory input is transformed, reduced, elaborated, stored, recovered, and used. It is concerned with these processes even when they operate in the absence of relevant stimulation, as in images and hallucinations.

Pertinent to our search, scientists define *perception* (17 p. 161) (18 p. 123) as a process that organisms use to organize, identify and interpret sensation in order to create representations of the surrounding environment.

> Perception is the process by which organisms interpret and organize sensation to produce a meaningful experience of the world.

***

> Perception is the organization, identification and interpretation of a sensation in order to form a mental representation.

Castaneda (1 p. 73) used a definition of *perception* that is entirely consistent with these scientific descriptions.

> Human beings apprehend energy at large and turn it into sensory data. Then they interpret these sensory data into the world of everyday life. This interpretation is what we call perception.

These definitions of perception are particularly important since the stated goal of the shamanic practices, advocated by Castaneda and his cohorts, is to enhance perception and expand awareness. Therefore, the processes involved in perception are key to assessing the ability of the practices to enhance the practitioner's perceptual ability.

If we examine perception in greater detail, we immediately realize that the cognitive processes and abilities associated with perception are vitally important because they facilitate the apprehension and interpretation of environmental energy, resulting in *experiential data* that is beneficial to survival. In other words, perception makes us aware of the world around us, thereby aiding our survival. Here, the phrase *experiential data* refers to any impressions, or qualia, resulting from personal experience, specifically including sensory data (i.e. sights, sounds, bodily sensations, etc.), as well as cognitive sensations (i.e. thoughts, feelings, images, dreams, memories, etc.) since these too are experienced. Apprehension refers to the detection and transformation of energy (or variations in energy) enabling experience. Interpretation refers to isolating, extracting or combining *experiential data* and assigning meaning to it. 'Beneficial to survival', means that through experience we acquire knowledge about the environment, knowledge that can increase the chances for individual survival and/or survival of the species.

Essentially, the principal cognitive functions associated with perception can be represented as three general process-abilities (see highlighted functions in Figure 1). Baars (19 p. 240) provides an analogous diagram, "A functional framework", that illustrates similar components such as sensory processing, memory, attention and executive functions leading to actions and responses. While the functions in Figure 1 are general and classified by arbitrary demarcations, each definition remains consistent with common usage. In fact, the descriptor phrase, 'process-ability' implies: 'an ability to perform an activity, function or change which leads toward a particular result'. Therefore, the function or activity of these cognitive process-abilities, is to apprehend, organize and interpret the energy surrounding us 'toward the particular result' of coping with the environment, thereby aiding adaptation and survival. In essence, we must be able to perceive the world around us in order to interact with it. Furthermore, the ability to interpret sensations, and discriminate between danger and sustenance, is essential for the continued survival of the individual and the species. Simply put, perception can enhance survivability.

Figure 1 is a simplified diagram which highlights three central process-abilities associated with perception: memory, attention and volition. In essence, energy from the environment (internal and external) is rendered into sensation. Sensations activate memory and together they provide the data and the reference framework for identification and association. Sensations and memories, guided by the selectivity of attention, are emphasized, or not, and become the focus of awareness, or not. Finally, volition weighs the value of each perceptual possibility, consequently directing attention to allocate preference in accordance with interest, importance and value. Choice is enabled by the variety of sensations and the various possibilities for combination, interpretation and resultant behavior. Also, represented in the diagram is a feedback path from volition, which feeds-back "interest, importance and value" to influence and direct memory and attention. However, keep in mind that this is only a simplified description which is being used to illustrate important process-abilities associated with perception.

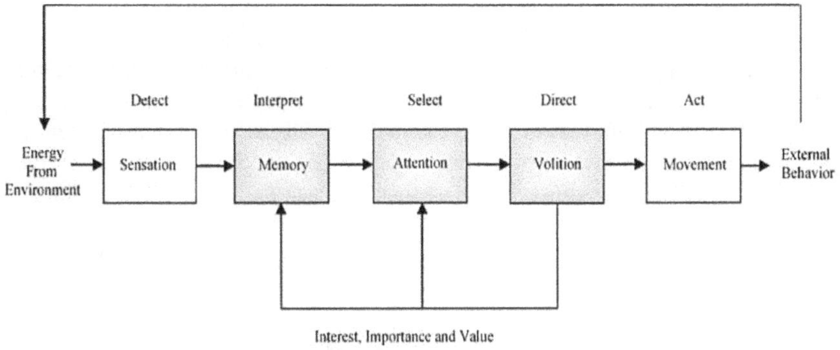

Figure 1 Diagram Illustrating Process-Abilities Associated with Perception

The process-abilities depicted in Figure 1 are illustrative of the cognitive processing associated with perception, and can be viewed as a reducing/organizing filter, with a substantial reduction and simplification of energy from the environment at each progressive stage. At the beginning (Figure 1, far left), energy from the environment presents an immense quantity of possibilities. The physical body and its sensory organs reduce the immensity of energy surrounding the human body to a scope that can be detected and represented by ordinary human sensation. Those countless sensations are in turn matched to a finite set of past experiences through personal memory and subsequently identified and organized, enabling attention to selectively filter and isolate pertinent information based on the importance established by our personal and social value systems. By the time the environmental energy reaches the executive process of volition, vast amounts of energy have been ignored, suppressed or generalized, and effectively reduced through exclusion, combination and conceptualization. The environmental energy has been effectively organized and structured by perception, leaving only modest, but useful, representations of the original immensity. The processes of organization, focalization and choice are critical to isolating relevant energy patterns and enabling effective interaction with specific aspects of the environment, ultimately guiding behavior and thus enabling adaptation and survival. In other words, perception allows us to receive energy from the environment and ignore energetic features of the world that *are not* important to us, so we can isolate and focus on the energetic features that *are* important to us.

As shown in Figure 1, the first process-ability associated with perception is sensation; the beginning of personal experience. Sensation is the detection of energy, generating experiential data which creates a link between perceived and perceiver; object and subject. Authentic sensation is <u>an actual transformation of energy</u> from the environment into electro-chemical energy. In biological terms, sensation is the conversion of various types of energy (or changes in energy), by sensory neurons, into electro-chemical information for transmission to other neurons. In other words, sensory neurons are *energy transducers*; literally converting energy from one form into another. For example, photoreceptors in the eye convert light energy (photons) into electro-chemical nerve signals that are transmitted to the brain. Chemoreceptors in the mouth and nose convert chemical energy into taste and smell sensations by responding to concentrations of various chemicals. Mechanoreceptors transform mechanical energy into the sensations of hearing and touch by responding to the mechanical energies of pressure and vibration. Proprioceptors, located throughout the muscles and tendons of the body, transform tensional energy into the sensations of body movement and position.

However, when various electro-chemical signals are produced by sensory neurons, in response to energy, the resultant neuronal signals do not convey any explicit information. Identification and characterization of the energy occurs when sensations stimulate memory. For example, audible sounds are simply waves of vibrating molecules that stimulate auditory nerves. It is memory that identifies and classifies the sound based on previous experience. As Edelman (20 p. 137) describes it,

> …extrinsic signals convey information not so much in themselves, but by virtue of how they modulate the intrinsic signals exchanged within a previously experienced neural system.

Memory is the second process-ability illustrated in Figure 1, and is generally understood as the ability to store and recall information and experience. Memory provides the function of persistence which facilitates interpretation by enabling recall, identification, association and comparison. Many scientists believe that memory is a vast network of neural structures and associations, with stronger connections existing between related items, and more connections, sometimes called elaborations, existing between familiar items. Memory can retain and recall simple facts, sensations, moods, or complete episodes of personal experience.

According to neuroscientists, memories are essentially patterns of neural association that are formed through personal experience. Hebbian Theory describes *learning*, which is the formation of new memories, as a process where, "Neurons that fire together, wire together". In other words, when sensations arise that repeatedly or consistently cause a set of neurons (cell-assemblies) to fire together, then there is an increase in the association between those cell-assemblies and those cells "wire together". One consequence of learning is that as sensations arise during an experience, the memories most closely associated with those sensations are also activated, effectively interpreting the sensations by relating them to memories of previous experiences. This important idea is worth repeating:

Sensations arising from environmental energy are identified, organized and interpreted, by memories previously associated with those sensations.

For example, our memory of "apple" is activated when our senses respond to the features associated with "apple" such as the size, shape, color, taste, smell, or when we imagine an apple or hear the word. An individual, such as a child, that has no experience of "apple", has no memory to associate with the sensations of "apple". But, over time, repeated exposure to "apple", and other related objects, enables the child to develop complex associations between the sensations and qualia associated with the experience of "apple". In this way, memory unites current sensations of "apple" with prior sensory experiences, to interpret them. Consequently, memory plays an important role in perceiving the world around us, since it is our memories that identify and interpret energy from the environment.

It's interesting to note the various words we use, when we talk about memory. We use words such as *remember*, implying that there was previously a group of *members* that are now being brought back into their membership by *re-membering* them. The *members* of the group are energetic features that we previously extracted from the environment and retained in memory, and are now being brought back into membership. Other words such as: re-collect, re-call and re-mind also illustrate the same idea that we are collecting back together, or calling back, members or collections of features, that do not retain their unity as a concept or mental picture, until we initiate the action to gather them again into their previously established membership, collection, or assembly. For example, round and red are features that can be applied to countless perceptions, but these features are *collected*, or *membered*, again to perceive a red apple.

Additionally, scientific evidence, as well as our own personal experience, tell us that emotion plays a powerful role in the encoding process of memory. Simply put, we are more likely to remember emotional events than unemotional ones (21 pp. 725-733), not only because emotional events captivate and focus attention, but also because feelings provide a powerful and common thread for elaborating new memories, or associating existing memories. Importance and value, which are intimately related to emotional feelings, also demonstrate powerful effects on memory.

The effects that emotion and attention have on memory, play a significant role in adaptation and survival. Emotion interacts with attention to identify and favor the storage of important (value-laden) events over mundane events, effectively increasing the probability of formation, retention, and recollection of memories that contain crucial information. In other words, when something vitally important happens, we need to remember it. Unfortunately, emotions sometimes create influential memories out of experiences that are no longer useful, such as victims of trauma who experience Post Traumatic Stress Disorder (PTSD). Emotion, then is a powerful agent for influencing attention as well as constructing and retaining memories.

The third process-ability illustrated in Figure 1 is attention, and it is the focus and concentration of awareness. Neurologically, attention acts by *modulating* stimulus-induced electrical potentials (21 pp. 189-289). In other words, attention is thought to preferentially favor certain neuronal groups by enhancing the firing of select neurons or neuronal groups. In general, attention enables the management of sensation and memory by preferentially selecting and sustaining various sensations and remembrances to be attended. Without doubt sensation and memory are necessary for perception, but it is attention that enables sensation and memory to be effectively utilized, by isolating and selecting relevant information, while discarding or ignoring irrelevant information.

Additionally, the word "attention" hints at its ability to "selectively bind" or "assemble" through its association with the Latin *tendere*, meaning to stretch, draw tight or bring under tension. From this perspective, attention can be seen as a *selecting ability* that preferentially binds, unites, or assembles, specific neuronal groups or coalitions, and their resultant concepts, by bringing them into prominence over others.

As previously noted, concentration and focus are the essential abilities of attention. Without the facilities of selection and exclusion imparted by attention, we would be confused, dazed and scatter-brained. William James (22 p. 103) has famously characterized the process of attention as being selective and exclusive.

> Every one knows what attention is. It is the taking possession by the mind, in clear and vivid form, of one out of what seem several simultaneously possible objects or trains of thought. Focalization, concentration, of consciousness are of its essence. It implies withdrawal from some things in order to deal effectively with others, and is a condition which has a real opposite in the confused, dazed, scatterbrained state which in French is called distraction and Zerstreutheit in German.

Like a specially trained sentinel, attention can apply greater significance to some stimuli while ignoring others. Experiences that are meaningful, or more highly valued, seem to demand some quantity of attention to remain vigilant and ready to receive and respond to valued information. This is most commonly exemplified by the so-called "cocktail party effect", which enables a person to focus on one specific conversation out of many, or suddenly hear their name, without intentionally listening for it, in the midst of a crowded room filled with dozens of voices and background noises. The value-based, interest-driven selectivity of attention (21 pp. 219-230) (23) (24) demonstrates two consequences associated with the power of 'interest, importance and value'. First, when we decide something has value, or we give it elevated importance, we are literally priming our attention to capture information relevant to that specific concern – we are on the lookout for it. Second, as James (22 p. 103) points out, when we allocate or use attentional resources to focus on value-laden information, we do so at the cost of excluding other information from awareness. "Paying attention" to specific aspects of the environment is like tuning a television to a specific channel, in that we become clearly aware of the details of the program on that channel, but we also become unaware of the programs running on all the other channels.

Personal experience also teaches us that a variety of things can attract attention. Even when we are actively directing our attention, extraneous sensations can distract it; draw it away; or divert it from its intended focus. For example, some sensations that can attract attention are; things that are abrupt, loud, bright, shiny or flashing, such as police and fire vehicles. Pain and discomfort can also readily attract our attention. This characteristic of attention is compatible with enhancing survival, since abrupt changes in the environment, or the sensation of pain, should be addressed with high priority in order to increase the chances of avoiding potential danger.

Volition, or intention, is the fourth process-ability of perception illustrated in Figure 1, and it intertwines and unites the previous three processes with choice and will, rendering value and judgment into a force that guides interpretation and drives action. Values are established through our personal experiences, via interaction with the external world and socialization. As we live our lives, we develop a system of judgments and we accumulate an inventory of values which enables us to determine the relative level of importance, interest or aversion, we have toward everything we encounter. It is our inventory of values that we rely on, whenever we need to make a choice. Choices are generally based on achieving the highest value, or reward, as determined by our personal value system.

Neurocognitively speaking, volition and intention are called *executive functions*, which includes unifying our motivations, desires, feelings and cognitive abilities toward actions that we prefer to be realized. "Executive function involves an individual's ability to conceptualize, to think independently, and to utilize self-control, self-direction, and flexibility." (25 p. 57)

Volition appears to allow independent decisions, but most of the time, our so-called 'choices' are actually derived from a lifetime of habits, judgments and learned values. True volition emerges beyond the boundaries of habit and interest, and stands firm, in the form of intent, or will, even when it contradicts our inventory of values. Volition is more than just the habitual engagement of value, interest and importance. As William James (26 p. 559) points out, pain, pleasure, instinct, emotion and habit, all "drive other thoughts from consciousness at the same time that they instigate their own characteristic 'volitional' effects." In other words, what sometimes appears to be an act of volition is not really an act of volition, since the act is driven not by "free will" or impartiality, but by habit, simply because habit makes it the "steadfast occupancy of consciousness" and the "steadfast occupancy of consciousness" is the essential phenomenon of volition. James (26 p. 558) makes clear that, in this way, interest, rather than volition, can control attention and consequently determine action.

> If one must have a single name for the condition upon which the impulsive quality of objects depends, one had better call it their *interest.* 'The interesting' is a title which covers not only the pleasant and the painful, but also the morbidly fascinating, the tediously haunting, and even the simply habitual, inasmuch as the attention usually travels on habitual lines, and what-we-attend-to and what-interests-us are synonymous terms.

Ultimately, James (26 pp. 561-562) exposes the true nature of volition and its affiliation with attention when he writes:

> … attention with effort is all that any case of volition implies. The essential achievement of will … is to attend to a difficult object and hold it fast before the mind."
>
> Effort of attention is thus the essential phenomenon of will.

Schwartz (27 p. 325), a psychiatrist studying volition and its ability to cause physical changes to neural pathways in the brain, elegantly summarizes his agreement with James that the effective role of will is 'sustaining the contents of attention'.

> The essential achievement of the will is to attend to one object and hold it clear and strong before the mind, letting all others – its rivals for attention and subsequent action – fade away like starlight swamped by the radiance of the sun.

As Figure 1 attempts to illustrate, in a very real sense, our view of the world around us is largely determined by our system of values, reflected from the environment as though by a mirror. This is worth repeating: our perception of the world around us, is largely a reflection of ourselves, since the environment merely reflects our own value system back to us, like a mirror. Simply put, our view of the world is constructed predominantly from the things that have interest, importance and value for us; **we see in the world, what we are on the look-out for**. Impressions from the world that have little interest, importance or value to us, go largely or completely unnoticed. James (22 p. 515) echoed this sentiment when he notes the interaction between interest and attention, and their powerful effect on perception.

> ... personal interest probably acts through attention and not in any immediate or specific way. A distinction in which we have a practical stake is one which we concentrate our minds upon and which we are on the look-out for. We draw it frequently, and we get all the benefits of so doing ... Where, on the other hand, a distinction has no practical interest, where we gain nothing by analyzing a feature from out of the compound total of which it forms a part, we contract a habit of leaving it unnoticed, and at last grow callous to its presence.

Cognitive processes, such as memory, attention and volition, play essential roles in our perception of the world around us, and yet they are strongly influenced by the value system we inherit. Castaneda identifies the socialization process as a significant factor in shaping our perception of the world. Essentially, the three cognitive process-abilities: memory, attention and volition, that allow us to perceive and 'know' the world around us, are the same processes that can restrict or distort our view of the world. Castaneda (11 p. 49) (15 p. xviii) (28 p. 5) and Abelar (2 p. viii) make clear that our perception of the world is learned through our culture and society. In other words, from the moment we start learning, we are taught what we are supposed to 'be on the lookout for', what things are important, valuable and interesting. In this way, our culture and society help to create our system of values.

We like to think we perceive the world as it actually is, and we generally believe that we perceive the world in all its fullness, and that very little escapes our perception. But, in agreement with Castaneda, James (22 p. 288) notes, our cognitive processes have been socially trained to extract specific features from the environment in order to construct a very specific view; a view that we have inherited from preceding generations; a view "which our ancestors and we, by slowly cumulative strokes of choice, have extricated out of ... the primordial chaos".

> The mind, in short, works on the data it receives very much as a sculptor works on his block of stone. In a sense, the statue stood there from eternity. But there were a thousand different ones beside it, and the sculptor alone is to thank for having extricated this one from the rest. Just so the world of each of us, howsoever different our several views of it may be, all lay embedded in the primordial chaos of sensations, which gave the mere matter to the thought of all of us indifferently. We may, if we like, by our reasonings unwind things back to that black and jointless continuity of space and moving clouds of swarming atoms which science calls the only real world. But all the while the world we feel and live in

> will be that which our ancestors and we, by slowly cumulative strokes of choice, have extricated out of this, like sculptors, by simply rejecting certain portions of the given stuff. Other sculptors, other statues from the same stone! Other minds, other worlds from the same monotonous and inexpressive chaos! My world is but one in a million alike embedded, alike real to those who may abstract them. How different must be the worlds in the consciousness of ant, cuttlefish, or crab!

Even though we have taken an analytical approach and decomposed perception into various process-abilities, we should recognize that the true power of perception emerges in the binding together of energetic features of our immediate environment and synthesizing the separate elements into the seamless and coherent view of the world we see before us. Murre (29 p. 222) describes the binding process of consciousness from a neural perspective:

> Binding is the process that determines the structure of representations in the brain. During the binding process neurons become bound into a coherent representation corresponding to actual objects or concepts in the world.

Neuroscientists that study consciousness have developed theories to explain how various neural processes may contribute to awareness. According to the theories based on *neuronal coalitions*, neurons are able to dynamically assemble into coherent groups, even though each neuron, or neuronal group, maintains its activation with a particular energetic feature. Specifically, neurons, or groups of neurons, learn and maintain highly specialized responses to distinct stimuli. Furthermore, each neuron, or group of neurons, can join to cooperate with other groups of neurons, to create highly differentiated, yet integrated assemblies (20). Conscious perception is then theorized to occur by dynamically activating a multitude of specialized neurons, each cooperating in a unified manner to construct a conscious view of a specific, or remembered scene. For every scene perceived, a unique combination of neuronal groups is dynamically assembled by either incorporating or excluding, through competition, various groups of neurons necessary to interpret or recollect the scene. These ensembles of neurons, like consciousness, are highly adaptive and constantly changing and shifting, depending on the environment.

Consciousness theories based on neuronal groups or coalitions, illustrate a biological processing strategy that is both economical and flexible (30). Processing is economical in the sense that specific neurons can remain responsive to elementary features of the environment, and yet participate in a multitude of different assemblies. For example, the neurons or neuronal group(s) that respond to 'red' can be incorporated into any perception or memory requiring 'red' and excluded when 'red' is not present. Furthermore, the theories of neuronal groups and coalitions also reflect the highly flexible nature of consciousness, since neuronal groups can be assembled to perceive scenes that have never been experienced before. Indeed, the possible combinations of unique neuronal assemblies are essentially limitless.

The idea that consciousness, or awareness, is a process that literally constructs the world around us, is not without support in the scientific community. Nobel laureate Gerald Edelman (20 p. 217) succinctly captures the essential function of consciousness in his ground-breaking work on the Theory of Neuronal Group Selection.

> [biologically based epistemology] then proposes that the efficacious role of consciousness is to construct an informative scene ("the remembered present") that connects present reality to the past value-ridden history of each individual conscious animal.

In this excerpt, Edelman and Tononi point out three significant characteristics of consciousness; 1) it constructs an "informative scene", 2) present reality - "the remembered present"- is a scene constructed from an individual's personal experience/history and 3) the history of each individual is laden with value. These are extremely powerful and insightful ideas which not only garner support from modern neuroscience, but also strongly resonate with the philosophical rationale underlying the methods prescribed by Castaneda.

Specifically, Edelman and Tononi (20) describe a biological theory which relies on dynamic groups of neurons to explain how consciousness constructs an informative scene from signals in the world. Similarly, Castaneda (15 p. xvi) wrote that the shaman of ancient Mexico believed the awareness associated with each individual has an *assemblage point*, where the "flux of energy at large" is turned into sensory data and then interpreted as "the world that surrounds us". Thus, in the lingo of neuroscience, 'consciousness constructs an informative scene', and in the lingo of shaman, 'awareness assembles the world around us'.

Edelman and Tononi (20 p. 105) also point out that value-based memory, resulting from past experience, plays a central role in enabling an individual to interpret the present environment. In fact, the on-going interpretation of the present environment, based on personal memory, has been aptly named, the "remembered present", by Edelman. According to Edelman and Tononi, not only do neural mechanisms exist which enable personal value systems to connect to memory regions of the brain, but those value systems also provide strong constraints on memory.

Abelar (2 p. 74) wrote extensively about the practice of *Recapitulation*, and expressed the idea that we are like "a giant memory warehouse" which holds all the "feelings, ideas, mental dialogues and behavior patterns" which have been stored within us as a personal inventory. In essence, our perception is constrained by our memory because we can only select and use items from our "memory warehouse", therefore we are limited in what is "possible and permissible to see". Indeed, Abelar (2 p. 73) unmistakably echoes the sentiment of Edelman's phrase, "the remembered present", when she writes "the world is a huge screen of memories". In both expressions, the authors make clear that **our perception of the present environment is determined by the reactivation of our memories**.

In this chapter, we have described perception and briefly examined the central cognitive processes involved in perceiving – memory, attention and volition – because these processes are key to understanding how the shamanic practices can enhance the practitioner's perception. We have also discussed physical correlates of perception, establishing a connection between the body and perception, because it is the physical body that enables the shamanic practices to affect perceptual changes. As the practices, advocated by Castaneda, are explored in the following chapters, we will present evidence of their power to create changes in the process-abilities associated with perception. Specifically, we will present and discuss a collection of scientific research, and other relevant material, which support the conclusion that the practices are conducive to enhancing perception and expanding the scope of individual awareness.

References

1. **Castaneda, Carlos.** *Magical Passes: The Practical Wisdom of the Shamans of Ancient Mexico.* New York, NY, USA : HarperCollins Publishers, Inc., 1998.

2. **Abelar, Taisha.** *The Sorcerers' Crossing: A Woman's Journey.* New York, NY, USA : Penguin Books USA Inc., 1992.

3. **Donner, Florinda.** *Being-In-Dreraming: An Initiation into the the Sorcerer's World.* New York, NY, USA : HarperCollins Publishers, Inc., 1991.

4. *Neural correlates of consciousness.* **Rees, Geraint.** New York, NY, USA : Annals of the New York Academy of Sciences, 2013, Vols. 1296: 4-10.

5. *Neural Correlates of Consciousness in Humans.* **Rees, Geraint and Kreiman, Gabriel and Koch, Christof.** New York, NY, USA : NATURE REVIEWS NEUROSCIENCE, 2002, Vols. 3: 261-270.

6. *The Neural Correlates of Consciousness: An Update.* **Tononi, Giulio and Koch, Christof.** New York, NY, USA : Annals of the New York Academy of Sciences, 2008, Vols. 1124: 239-261.

7. *Neurophenomenology Integrating Subjective Experience and Brain Dynamics in the Neuroscience of Consciousness.* **Lutz, Antoine and Thompson, E.** (9–10): 31–52, Exeter, UK : Journal of Consciousness Studies, 2003, Vol. 10.

8. **Foulkes, David.** *Children's Dreaming and the Development of Consciousness.* Cambridge, MA, USA : Harvard University Press, 1999.

9. **Leclercq, Michel, Zimmermann, Peter and van Zomeren, Adriaan H.** *Applied Neuropsychology of Attention Theory, Diagnosis and Rehabilitation.* New York, NY, USA : Psychology Press, 2002.

10. **Kaplan, R. M., & Saccuzzoo, D. P.** *Psychological Testing: Principles, Applications, and Issues., 8th Ed.* Stanford, CT, USA : Jon-David Hague, Cengage Learning , 2005.

11. **Castaneda, Carlos.** *The Fire from Within.* New York, NY, USA : Simon and Schuster, 1984.

12. —. *The Power of Silence: Further Lessons of don Juan.* New York, NY, USA : Washington Square Press / Simon & Schuster Inc., 1987.

13. **Grinspoon, Lester and Bakalar, James B.** *Psychedelic Drugs Reconsidered.* New York, NY, USA : The Lindesmith Center, 1998.

14. **Eliade, Mircea.** *Shamanism: Archaic Techniques of Ecstasy.* Princeton , NJ, USA : Princeton University Press, 1964.

15. **Castaneda, Carlos.** *The Teachings of don Juan: A Yaqui Way of Knowledge - Deluxe 30th Anniversary Edition.* Los Angeles, CA, USA : University of California Press, 1998.

16. **Neisser, Ulric.** *Cognitive Psychology: Classic Edition.* New York, NY, USA : Psychology Press,Taylor & Francis, 2014.

17. **Lindsay, Peter and Norman, Donald A.** *Human Information Processing: An Introduction to Psychology.* New York, NY, USA : Academic Press, Inc., 1977.

18. **Schacter, Daniel L., Gilbert, Daniel T. and Wegner, Daniel M.** *Psychology.* New York, NY, USA : Worth Publishers, 2009.

19. **Baars, Bernard J. and Gage, Nicole M.** *Cognition, Brain, and Consciousness* . Burlington, MA, USA : Academic Press / Elsevier Ltd., 2007.

20. **Edelman, Gerald M. and Tononi, Giulio.** *A Universe of Consciousness : How Matter Becomes Immagination.* New York, NY, USA : Basic Books / Perseus Books Group, 2000.

21. **Gazzaniga, Michael S.** *The Cognitive Neurosciences.* Cambridge, MA, USA : The MIT Press, 2009.

22. **James, William.** *The Principles of Psychology Vol1* . Mineola, NY, USA : Dover Publications Inc., 1950.

23. *A value-driven mechanism of attentional selection.* **Anderson, Brian A.** 7, 1–16, Rockville, MD, USA : Association for Research in Vision and Ophthalmology, 2013, Vol. Journal of Vision 13.

24. *Value-driven attentional capture in the auditory domain.* **Anderson, Brian A.** Madison, WI, USA : The Psychonomic Society, 2015, Vol. Attention Perception & Psychophysics 78 .

25. **Hof, Patrick R. and Mobbs, Charles V.** *Functional Neurobiology of Aging.* New York, NY, USA : Academic Press, 2001.

26. **James, William.** *The Principles of Psychology Vol 2.* Mineola,NY, USA : Dover Publications Inc., 1950.

27. **Schwartz, Jeffrey M.** *The Mind and the Brain: Neuroplasticity and the Power of Mental Force.* New York,NY, USA : ReganBooks / HarperCollins Publishers Inc., 2003.

28. **Castaneda, Carlos.** *The Wheel of TIme: The Shamans of Ancient Mexico, Their Thoughts about Life, Death and the Universe.* Los Angeles, CA, USA : LA Eidolona Press, 1998.

29. **Zimmer, Hubert, Mecklinger, Axel and Lindenberger, Ulman.** *Handbook of Binding and Memory: Perspectives from Cognitive Neuroscience.* New York, NT, USA : Oxford University Press Inc., 2006.

30. *Integrated information theory of consciousness: an updated account.* **Tononi, Giulio.** Pisa, Italy : PisaUniversity Press, 2012, Vols. Archives Italiennes de Biologie 150: 290-326.

CHAPTER 2

Left and Right Awareness

****

In addition to perception, it is also necessary to explore the separation of awareness into left and right divisions, because references to left and right awareness occur throughout the works of Castaneda and Abelar, signifying them as important concepts in the expansion of awareness. Interestingly, decades of research in neuroscience, particularly studies with split-brain patients, have uncovered that indeed human beings do possess two different, and relatively independent, consciousnesses apparently arising from the left and right hemispheres of the brain. Pederson (1 p. 19) succinctly affirms the scientific importance of this finding by noting that Sperry, et al, were awarded the Nobel Prize for their historic discovery.

> In 1980 a Nobel Prize was awarded to Professor Roger Sperry of the California Institute of Technology for his work on identifying specific functions of the brain which were lateralized either to the left or right hemispheres. He concluded from his work that human beings consist of two people in the same body, he says:
>
> [We are] … two separate spheres of conscious awareness, that is two separate conscious entities running parallel in the same bony cranium each with its own sensations, perception, cognitive processes, learning experience, memories, and so on.

Pederson (1 p. 45) also discusses the work of Vadim Deglin, a leading Russian neurophysiologist who used unilateral Electro-Convulsive Therapy (ECT) to characterize and describe the *left hemisphere person* and the *right hemisphere person*. Deglin's research led him to concur with Sperry's conclusion that we are indeed two separate conscious entities in the same bony cranium. And while significant differences do exist between the left and right hemispheres of the brain, we believe Castaneda's reference to left and right awareness refers to different *modes* of awareness that are substantially, but not exclusively, determined by hemispheric laterality.

Castaneda (2 p. 138) tells us that the Shamans of ancient Mexico recognized that human beings are "composed of two complete functioning bodies, one on the left and one on the right", and they saw that fundamental division as an opportunity to effectively employ the left body in reaching their ultimate goals.

These "two separate conscious entities", each with its own cognitive processes and perceptions, play a key role in the shaman's goal of expanding awareness. Abelar (3 p. 42) (3 p. 61) (3 p. 224) gives the first indication of this objective – shifting awareness from the left to the right side of the head – when she describes "the abstract flight" as a shift in awareness from the left to the right side of the head.

As the above references demonstrate, a shift from right-side awareness to left-side awareness is described in various ways. For example, Abelar refers to it as the *abstract flight*, the *sorcerer's crossing*, the shift from the left side to the right side (shifting daily awareness to the double), as well as bringing the double into daily awareness (shifting from the right side to the left side). The terminology can not only be confusing because of the various phrases and descriptions used, but also because, for the most part, the left brain controls the right half of the body and the right brain controls the left half of the body, with the exception of the head. However, Castaneda (2 p. 143) attempts to simplify the confusion by using the terminology of "left and right bodies" and specifies that it is different from the terminology of "left and right *sides of the* body", stating that for the shamanic movement sequences he prescribed, "it is recommended to adopt the division of left and right bodies, rather than left and right sides of the body". Castaneda (2 p. 143) preferred the terminology, *left and right body,* to avoid confusing the *right side* of the head/brain with the *right side of the body*, since the *right side* of the head/brain is predominantly associated with the *left side of the body* and vice versa.

Furthermore, during his training in the practice of shamanic 'dreaming', Castaneda (4 p. 258) confirms that it is the *order of predominance* that shifts between right and left side awareness, in the special state called 'dreaming'. In other words, the left side awareness becomes dominant over the normally dominant right side awareness.

Castaneda (5 p. 116) (4 p. 163) also explains that the shaman's philosophy divides the energy of man into the "tonal" and the "nagual", revealing a variety of names that shamans use for each division. Specifically, the "tonal" is also referred to as the "right side", "normal awareness", "this world", the "known" and the "first attention", while the "nagual" is referred to as the "left side", "heightened awareness", the "other world", the "unknown", and the "second attention".

According to Castaneda (6 p. 270) (6 p. 266) (6 p. 122) (6 p. 141), the tonal is "that indescribable unknown filled with order", "where all the unified organization exists" and the nagual is, "the unspeakable", "that indescribable void that contains everything".

Employing different terminology, Gowan (7 pp. 3-4) perhaps lends further insight into the nagual, referring to "that indescribable void that contains everything" as the "numinous element" and the "mysterium tremendum".

> It is difficult, if not impossible, to state exactly what the numinous element is. The Aztecs called it "Smoking Mirror" which indicates its reflective impersonal aspect. It appears to us as fluidic and watery, without form, and hence in this sense "void." The Hindus call it "the clear light of the Void."

The association between the right/left side and the tonal/nagual are also evident in the record of Castaneda's experiences. Some examples of this include; the apprentices on the bridge (4 p. 100) were "compelled to cross from the right side, the tonal, to the left side, the nagual", Castaneda was always flanked to his right by his teacher (the tonal guide) and to his left by his benefactor (the nagual guide) (6 p. 248), Castaneda's awareness was split in half using dichotic listening (6 p. 183) with the teacher on his right and the benefactor on his left, and Castaneda's imperative to 'remember his left side' (4 p. 57) which held the memories of his excursions into the nagual.

Similar to Castaneda's claim that different teachers and teaching techniques were used for his left and right-side awareness, Pederson (1 p. 39) notes that the professional tennis coach, Tim Gallwey, refrained from verbal instruction (left hemisphere teaching) and primarily used visual images (right hemisphere teaching), because of the right hemisphere's superior ability in the spatial processing tasks required for playing tennis. Likewise, a popular art teacher, Betty Edwards, utilized teaching techniques that were designed to activate the right hemisphere of her students – a cognitive shift method – that produced outstanding results in her students and instigated change in art schools throughout the world. Additionally, because the right hemisphere develops earlier than the left, young children are more effectively taught early language, social and fine motor skills using right hemisphere learning styles such as song, rhyme and gesture. Ample evidence supports Castaneda's claim that each hemisphere is more responsive to specialized teaching styles.

Castaneda (8 p. 167) directly states that he understood his teacher's descriptions as metaphor for the "dominance of the left hemisphere of the brain over the right" hemisphere.

Indeed, McGilchrist (9 pp. 17-18, 42) asserts that part of the corpus callosum – the primary neural tissue connecting the left and right hemispheres – has been found to be inhibitory. McGilchrist (9 pp. 27, 174-175) goes even further and generalizes the two forms of attention which neuroscience equates with the two hemispheres. The left hemisphere embodies a narrow, self-focused attention, while the right hemisphere embodies a broad attention, open and connected to the immediate environment. Furthermore, the left hemisphere employs language and abstraction to create a static, self-reflective world filled with the known. On the other hand, the right hemisphere is more directly connected to the environment and aware of its constant flow and change.

In fact, McGilchrist's (9 p. 6) seminal book, *The Master and His Emissary*, is based on the concept that the *Emissary* (left hemisphere -right body, self-focused) has usurped control over the *Master* (right hemisphere -left body, the world apart from the self). And unfortunately, the left-hemisphere (the Emissary) is leading western civilization into dark territory.

> Here I suggest that it is as if the left hemisphere, which creates a sort of self-reflexive virtual world, has blocked off the available exits, the ways out of the hall of mirrors, into a reality which the right hemisphere could enable us to understand.

McGilchrist's (9 p. 6) concern about the increasing difficulties associated with the "relentless growth of self-consciousness" as well as his characterization of the right-body attention as narrow and self-concerned, both resonate with the shaman's sentiment regarding self-importance. Castaneda (10 p. 37) made it clear that shaman regard self-importance as a "supreme enemy" and "the nemesis of mankind". In this light, "losing self-importance" - reducing self-focus - can be seen as a strategy to aid in a shift of attention away from the *first attention* of the right-body(left hemisphere) and toward the *second attention* of the left-body(right hemisphere).

Indeed, McGilchrist (9 p. 65) offers some evidence of the biological energy consumed by the self, pointing out that one area of the brain – the precuneus – is strongly connected to the sense of self, and is nearly always active, except in self-less states of consciousness.

Regarding the two separate spheres of conscious awareness, McGilchrist (9 pp. 33, 39) offers anatomical evidence that supports the notion of two different types of attention; one narrow and focused, the other broad and open. Specifically, the hemispheres differ in the way in which neurons are predominantly connected, noting that the right hemisphere contains more white matter, indicating the presence of myelination that facilitates rapid signaling <u>across</u> regions. In contrast,

In one particular study, Weis (18) tells us that hemispheric inhibition is reduced when sex hormone levels rise.

> Imaging data show that in women the inhibitory influence of the dominant on the nondominant hemisphere is reduced with rising levels of sex hormones in the course of the menstrual cycle. Apart from modulating interhemispheric inhibition, sex hormones also seem to change functional organization within hemispheres.

According to Castaneda (11 pp. 47,163), it appears that shaman were aware of the periodic changes in female brain chemistry and its concomitant changes in functional organization and cognition, and they strove to use it to their advantage. In support of the claim that "days before her period a woman can open that crack [between the worlds]" we find that during the days just prior to menses, hormone levels (progesterone and estradiol) are at a maximum and, according to Weis (18), interhemispheric inhibition is at a minimum. In addition, interhemispheric inhibition quickly returns when those hormone levels begin to rapidly fall as the 28-day cycle comes to an end and menstruation begins. Synthesizing this information, we can theorize that this unique set of circumstances might enable a female practitioner to bring the uninhibited cognition of the right hemisphere into union with the left hemisphere, creating a cognitive state similar to Abelar's "bringing the ethereal part of us, the double, into our daily awareness" or Castaneda's 'dreaming' experience, which resulted in merging the "right and left awareness into one in which the order of predominance has been switched and the left has gained supremacy."

In this particular example, we find that the goal of shaman - to capitalize on the menstrual cycle to facilitate the transfer of awareness from the right body to the left body - garners support from scientific studies because hormonal and concomitant cognitive changes do occur during the menstrual cycle. Specifically, the rapid decrease in hormone levels prior to menses, might provide an opportunity to combine the awareness of the left body and the right body, in a manner that temporarily switches the usual order of dominance. There appears to be adequate evidence indicating that the hemispheric inhibition of the dominant hemisphere is altered during the menstrual cycle, with rapid changes occurring just prior to menses.

Thus far we have examined a variety of scientific evidence documenting the separation of left and right body awareness that results in "two separate conscious entities". Additionally, we have indicated that several methods and practices described by Castaneda appear to enable or capitalize on the separation in awareness, signifying it as an important concept in the development of awareness. We believe that McGilchrist (9 p. 6) captures the essence of the shaman's goal - the enhancement of perception and awareness – when he writes;

> … the left hemisphere, which creates a sort of self-reflexive virtual world, has blocked off the available exits, the ways out of the hall of mirrors, into a reality which the right hemisphere could enable us to understand.

Furthermore, McGilchrist (9 p. 173) appears to echo the shaman's sentiment that it is the right hemisphere (left body) that can provide an avenue to escape "the hall of mirrors", through its broad, vigilant attention and creativity, by *lifting the veil of familiarity*. It is in the left body awareness where perceptual possibilities exist. It is the left body awareness (right hemisphere) that facilitates access to the nagual.

However, as Abelar (3 p. xiii) and Castaneda (4 p. 166) (6 p. 240) make clear, awareness of the right and left body is necessary for "a sober, pragmatic, new way of perceiving." The "tonal is the organizer of the world … setting the chaos of the world in order" by re-presenting the *intensity* of the nagual in a linear, sequential, clear and precise manner. The nagual is *all possibilities*, "that indescribable void that contains everything". The organizing ability of the tonal is necessary to make sense of the nagual, and yet it is the infinite potential of the nagual that makes everything possible. As Castaneda (2 p. 142) explains, both forms of awareness are necessary to reach our "totality".

In this chapter, we have explored the separation of awareness into left and right sides (the divided brain) and found that humans are indeed "two separate conscious entities running parallel in the same bony cranium". According to McGilchrist, mankind runs the danger of being imprisoned by the left hemisphere, trapped in a self-reflective hall of mirrors, closed off from the living world, with the right hemisphere offering the only avenue for escape. Likewise, Castaneda claims the fundamental division in awareness is critically important to the shamans' goal of expanding awareness beyond the confines of the daily world.

Both Castaneda and McGilchrist express concern that the dominance of the left hemisphere (right body) over the right hemisphere (left body), causes us to live our lives confined within the narrow boundaries of left hemisphere awareness, seeing *in the world,* just a reflection of what we already know. Only through right hemisphere awareness can we find the truly new and novel – the "primordial chaos" – the *mysterium tremendum*; only there, can we journey to Hennel's "secret edges of the mountain", and lift the *veil of familiarity*, to reveal the true grandeur of the universe.

In the following chapters, we present a collection of scientific research, and other relevant material, which support Castaneda's claims that the practices and methods he prescribed are conducive to enhancing perception and expanding personal awareness. We will specifically examine three essential practices:

Magical Passes, Recapitulation and Dreaming. Evidence is presented to support our hypothesis that each of these practices can enhance perception and expand awareness; 1) by improving various cognitive processes associated with perception through training; 2) by reducing attachments to the patterns and routines of ordinary daily awareness; and 3) by activating new possibilities for perception that lie beyond the boundaries of ordinary daily awareness.

References

1. **Pedersen, David L.** *Cameral Analysis: A Method of Treating Psychoneuroses Uisng Hypnosis.* New York, NY , USA : Routledge, 1994.

2. **Castaneda, Carlos.** *Magical Passes: The Practical Wisdom of the Shamans of Ancient Mexico.* New York, NY, USA : HarperCollins Publishers, Inc., 1998.

3. **Abelar, Taisha.** *The Sorcerers' Crossing: A Woman's Journey.* New York, NY, USA : Penguin Books USA Inc., 1992.

4. **Castaneda, Carlos.** *The Eagle's Gift.* New York, NY, USA : Pocket Books / Washinton Square Press / Simon & Schuster, 1981.

5. —. *The Fire from Within.* New York, NY, USA : Simon and Schuster, 1984.

6. —. *Tales of Power.* New York, NY, USA : Touchstone / Simon & Schuster, 1974.

7. **Gowan, John C.** *Trance, Art and Creativity.* Northridge, CA, USA : John Curtis Gowan, 1975.

8. **Castaneda, Carlos.** *The Active Side of Infinity.* New York, NY, USA : HarperCollins Publishers, 1998.

9. **McGilchrist, Iain.** *The Master and his Emissary; The Divided Brain and the Makingof the Western World.* NewHaven, CT, USA : Yale University Press, 2010.

10. **Castaneda, Carlos.** *The Art of Dreaming.* New York, NY, USA : First HarperPerennial / HarperCollins Publishers, 1994.

11. —. *The Second Ring of Power.* New York, NY, USA : Pocket Books / Washington Square Press / Simon & Schuster, 1977.

12. *Sex Differences and the Impact of Steroid Hormones on the Developing Human Brain.* **Neufang, S. , et al.** 19:464--473, Oxford, UK : Oxford University Press, 2009, Vol. Cerebral Cortex.

13. *Regional sex differences in grey matter volume are associated with sex hormones in the young adult human brain.* **Witte, A. V. , et al.** 49:1205–1212, Amsterdam, Netherlands : Elsevier, 2010, Vol. NeuroImage.

14. *Estradiol Modulates Functional Brain Organization during the Menstrual Cycle: An Analysis of Interhemispheric Inhibition.* **Weis, S. , et al.** 28:13401–13410, Washington, DC, USA : Society for Neuroscience, 2008, Vol. The Journal of Neuroscience.

15. *Functional cerebral asymmetries during the menstrual cycle: a cross-sectional and longitudinal analysis.* **Hausmann, M., et al.** 40: 808–816, Amsterdam, Netherlands : Elsevier Science Ltd, 2002, Vol. Neuropsychologia.

16. *Hemispheric asymmetry in spatial attention across the menstrual cycle.* **Hausmann, M.** 43:1559–1567, Amsterdam, Netherlands : Elsivier Science Ltd., 2005, Vol. Neuropsychologia .

17. *Transcallosal inhibition across the menstrual cycle: A TMS study.* **Hausmann, M. , et al.** 117; 26–32, Amsterdam, Netherlands : Elsevier Science Ltd, 2006, Vol. Clinical Neurophysiology .

18. *Sex Hormones: Modulators of Interhemispheric Inhibition in the Human Brain.* **Weis, S. , Hausmann, M.** 132-8, New Haven, CT, USA : Sage Publications, 2010, Vol. The Neuroscientist.

CHAPTER 3

Magical Passes®

****

Magical Passes are bodily movements and breaths that were apparently taught to Carlos Castaneda and Taisha Abelar by their respective teachers. According to Castaneda (1 p. 10), the *Magical Passes* were accidentally discovered by the shamans of ancient Mexico, when they probed a sensation of well-being that they experienced while holding certain body positions or when they moved their limbs in specific ways. The intense sensation of well-being drove them to uncover a complex series of movements and breaths that "when practiced, yielded them tremendous results in terms of mental and physical prowess". Castaneda (1 p. 7) decided to teach the *Magical Passes* to whoever wanted to learn them and subsequently developed a generic form of the *Magical Passes* that he named Tensegrity.

At first glance, the movements of a Tensegrity sequence might appear to resemble other movement systems such as Karate, Tai Chi, Qigong, Yoga, or even calisthenics. However, upon closer examination, the Tensegrity movements are unique in several ways. The sequences do not appear to be a form of martial arts, like a karate kata that is used to attack or defend against an opponent, even though Tensegrity sequences do incorporate kicks, strikes and blows. Yet, the movements are not simply callisthenic exercises because they do not resemble the usual strength activities such as sit-ups, pushups or jumping jacks. Instead, the choreography involves detailed positioning and motion of the torso, limbs, head, and occasionally the fingers, toes and eyes that are consistent with Castaneda's contention that they break up energy surrounding the body and redistribute it. Tensegrity also encompasses hundreds of series, where each series is made up of dozens of unique, but specific and detailed sequences of movements and breaths, ultimately offering a seemingly endless array of sequences to learn. In addition, Tensegrity incorporates lateralized movements that are unusual and complex motions that demand a high level of concentration, spatial-awareness, coordination and movement planning. Furthermore, Tensegrity has a recommended practice environment that is conducive to right hemisphere cognition. And finally, the movements – which alternate between tensing and relaxing – are sometimes performed vigorously, while at other times they are performed more slowly and deliberately.

First, Tensegrity is specifically different from other movement systems because the choreography, and its symbolism, are unique. The choreography matches the description given by Castaneda (1 pp. 15-16), since the movements do appear to be enacting a *redeployment of energy* by striking, dislodging, breaking up and grabbing unseen energy surrounding the body and redistributing it to the body's centers of vitality. Indeed, the movements distribute energy by: stimulating a diversity of nerves and muscles in an ever-changing sequence, increasing blood flow and oxygenation and massaging internal organs – the body's centers of vitality. In support of redistributing energy, the choreography embodies the intent of the *Magical Passes – to redeploy energy* – which is different from the intent of martial arts – to attack or defend. The embodiment of the gestures to strike, dislodge, break up and redistribute energy reinforces the desire and intent – especially in the right hemisphere – to reallocate physical and cognitive energy.

Second, there are hundreds of Tensegrity series, many consisting of long sequences of apparently unrelated movements that deliberately challenge and develop the practitioner's kinesthetic memory (1 p. 22). The substantial collection of Tensegrity series provides a seemingly endless collection of unusual and atypical movement sequences that demand the development and enhancement of various skills, such as kinesthetic memory, attentional focus and volitional engagement. The vast number and variety of the sequences, make Tensegrity unique and different from other movement systems, such as the Sun Salutations of Ashtanga Yoga and the 108 movements of Tai Chi, that are expressed by a limited number of fixed movements.

Third, unlike other physical sequences or exercises, Castaneda (1 p. 30) dictates that all *Magical Passes* begin with movement of the left body, followed by the right body, unless otherwise specified. Additionally, many of the movements are bilateral, cross-lateral or require immobility on the side of the body not performing the movement (1 p. 143).

Fourth, while there is no particular space required to practice Tensegrity, Castaneda (1 p. 25) recommends the movements be performed in an environment that is free from conversation, music, television and radio, as well as other "elements with which we are already thoroughly familiar."

And finally, Castaneda (1 p. 36) specifies the movements are to be performed "by contracting and relaxing the tendons and muscles of the body" – a technique similar to Progressive Muscle Relaxation, which is specifically used to reduce and relieve stress.

Castaneda (1 p. 4) asserts that the *Magical Passes* are the first step in redeploying our inherent energy, leading to an enhancement in physical and mental prowess.

We regard Castaneda's reference to the *redeployment of energy* as a singular phrase that represents the shaman's ultimate goal of developing and enhancing perception to enable awareness to shift into an arena of new possibilities. In essence, by following the path of the shamans of ancient Mexico, a practitioner can systematically redirect their energy toward the goal of shifting awareness into a new realm of possibilities. That shift in awareness, made possible by an enhancement of perception, is accomplished in the manner we have outlined as our hypothesis; 1) by improving various cognitive processes associated with perception through training; 2) by reducing attachments to the patterns and routines of *ordinary daily awareness*; and 3) by activating new possibilities for perception that lie beyond the boundaries of *ordinary daily awareness*.

Enhancing Perception

According to the first part of our hypothesis, *Magical Passes*, and its modern form Tensegrity, are one of the practices advocated by Castaneda, that, through regular training, can improve the essential process-abilities associated with perception, namely memory, attention and volition.

While peer reviewed research on Tensegrity is completely lacking at this time, we believe the sequences reasonably qualify as aerobic exercise, since they use large muscle groups repetitively, for a sustained amount of time. The "aerobic exercise" characterization of Tensegrity is particularly applicable since Castaneda (1 pp. 4,25,35,36) describes the practice of Tensegrity using phrases such as; "rigorous execution", "perspiring body", "Breath and breathing [are...] of supreme importance", and "As the body gets warmer, the tension should become greater and the length of time extended, but always in a moderate fashion.". Therefore, the scientific literature on aerobic exercise lends primary support for our hypothesis that Tensegrity is one of the practices that can foster the enhancement of perception and expansion of awareness.

A literature search on aerobic exercise and cognition, reveals significant evidence that supports Castaneda's claim of mental alertness and physical prowess. The physical benefits of regular exercise are abundant and well documented, so they will not be extensively reviewed here. However, the literature also provides substantial evidence that aerobic exercises, like Tensegrity practice, improves a variety of cognitive processes associate with perception, such as memory, attention and executive function (volition).

For example, Hillman (2) reviewed a number of meta-analyses examining the relationship between aerobic exercise and cognition and found statistically significant evidence that "in all studies, physical activity had a positive effect on cognition". The study specifically notes improvements in memory, attention and executive function.

Similarly, Smith (3) conducted a meta-analytic review of randomized control trials investigating aerobic exercise and neurocognitive performance, concluding that "Aerobic exercise training is associated with modest improvements in attention and processing speed, executive function, and memory…". Again, this review of multiple studies concludes that aerobic exercise produces specific improvements in processes associated with perception, including memory, attention and executive function (volition).

In another review of multiple scientific studies on the *effects of exercise on cognition*, Tomporowski (4) found that in the majority of studies, submaximal aerobic exercise was found to improve cognitive processing, including concentration, which requires both the *use of attentional resources* and the *executive function of volition* to direct and sustain mental focus.

Additionally, Colcombe (5) performed a meta-analysis of eighteen aerobic fitness studies to examine the hypothesis that aerobic fitness training enhances cognitive function in older adults. The conclusion, in agreement with similar studies, found that fitness training does indeed increase cognitive performance.

Furthermore, Gomez-Pinilla (6) provides a comprehensive account of the effects of exercise on the brain, reviewing animal studies, human studies and the underlying energetic molecular mechanisms that act to promote the cognitive improvements that result from aerobic exercise.

The statistically significant results of these numerous peer reviewed meta-analyses and scientific studies provide clear evidence that aerobic exercise improves various cognitive processes associated with perception; specifically, memory, attention and executive function. Contrasting the cognitive improvements resulting from aerobic exercise, many other studies have examined the progressive decline in cognitive ability that results from long term inactivity, often noting how even the simplest forms of exercise, such as walking, can result in slowing, or even reversing, cognitive decline.

Furthermore, Budde (7) found that *bilateral coordinative exercises*, enabled participants to be more effective in completing concentration and attention tasks. While both exercise groups in this study showed "enhanced attention and concentration performance", the coordinative exercise group showed significantly higher performance than the non-specific physical exercise group. The authors suggest that the motor complexity, associated with bilateral movement, stimulates and pre-activates "neuronal structures like the cerebellum and the frontal lobe [which] are responsible for coordination as well as cognition", and specifically, "...responsible for mediating functions like attention". Bilateral coordinative exercises incorporate the left and right sides of the body in simultaneous, coordinated movement, so this study is particularly relevant to Tensegrity, since bilateral coordinative movements are an integral component of Tensegrity sequences. This research supports the notion that bilateral coordinated movements, such as those used in Tensegrity, are particularly beneficial to enhancing attention and concentration.

Supporting evidence, for the role of the cerebellum in coordinating movement as well as coordinating shifts in attention, has been found in a study that includes patients with autism and patients with acquired cerebellar lesions. Courchesne (8) has theorized "that the human cerebellum is involved in the coordination of rapid attention shifts in a fashion analogous to its role in the coordination of movement". Courchesne (8) also cites significant anatomical evidence to implicate the cerebellum as an essential component in "... disengaging attention from one source and then moving and reengaging it on another. "

Research studies demonstrating the ability of *bilateral coordinative movement* to enhance attention and concentration, as well as those that implicate the cerebellum in coordinating shifts in attention, are particularly relevant to Tensegrity. According to Castaneda (9 p. 245), shaman "... sought the usefulness of the nagual by training their tonal to let go for a moment, so to speak, and then grab again", or in other words, to shift awareness from the *first attention* to the *second attention.* (a.k.a. shift awareness from *right side awareness* to *left side awareness*). In this regard, Tensegrity is an important undertaking for shaman practitioners because various studies indicate that *bilateral coordinative movement* and activation of the cerebellum can enhance the attentional ability to shift (let go) and reengage (grab on again).

Neurobiologically, the benefits of aerobic exercise, and consequently Tensegrity, include; neurogenesis – the creation of new neurons; angiogenesis – the creation of new blood vessels; and synaptogenesis – the creation of new synapses, each supporting the neural system and brain's intriguing ability to physically remodel itself – a process known as plasticity (8) (10). Consequently, Tensegrity practice can increase brain plasticity and therefore promote cognitive flexibility. In depth research implicates various growth factors, such as Brain-Derived Neurotrophic Factor (BDNF), in the development of new neurons, blood vessels and synapses in the hippocampus – a bilateral brain structure, considered part of the limbic system. The hippocampus is believed to play a primary role in memory.

Support for hippocampal improvements comes from a study extolling the perceptual improvements resulting from exercise. Erickson (11) noted that aerobic exercise training not only increased the size of the hippocampus, but the increase in hippocampal volume was directly related to improvements in memory performance.

Furthermore, some studies (12) (13) have concluded that *complex motor movements* – movements that require a high degree of attention, memory and motor difficulty – have a stronger effect on executive function and promote even greater neural growth in the hippocampus than simpler, repetitive movements (14).

Moreover, the memory benefits resulting from Tensegrity likely exceed those of ordinary aerobic exercise, because Tensegrity encompasses learning a considerable number of long sequences that involve not only complex movements, but also numerous details. The large number of Tensegrity series presents a seemingly endless supply of new sequences for practitioners to learn, requiring the regular use of concentration, executive function and kinesthetic memory. Interestingly, the right hemisphere plays a dominant role in kinesthetic processing (15) and according to Castaneda (1 p. 22), his teacher regarded the long sequences of *Magical Passes* as beneficial to the practitioner's kinesthetic memory.

Also, in an important long-term study, Woollett and Macquire (16) found that successful candidates, studying to become London taxi drivers, developed significant increases in hippocampal volume and concomitant changes in their memory. The candidates typically spent years cultivating an internal spatial representation of the complex layout of London's streets. We suggest that learning a large number of complex Tensegrity sequences (which require the use of spatial memory) would also repetitively engage the hippocampus and result in similar enhancements to memory.

And finally, according to leading brain fitness researcher, Michael Merzenich (17), "... BRAIN-LESS physical activity is much less useful for cognitive fitness development than physical activity that involves new experiences and continuous learning...[because] that drives continuous brain plasticity!". Therefore, the continuous learning opportunity, provided by the complexity and volume of Tensegrity series, appears to be more beneficial for cognitive fitness than simple repetitive physical activity.

Thus far, we have found support for the first part of our hypothesis, that Tensegrity can improve various cognitive processes associated with perception, by presenting significant evidence that aerobic exercise does indeed improve cognitive functions associated with perception; specifically, memory, attention and executive function. We have also made a case that Tensegrity, as a generic form of *Magical Passes*, qualifies as a form of aerobic exercise, because the movements:

1) use large muscle groups repetitively, for a sustained amount of time, 2) incorporate breath sequences and breathing techniques, and 3) call for sustained tension and rigorous execution. Additionally, we have cited research which highlight unique aspects of Tensegrity that particularly foster improvements in memory, attention, volition and brain plasticity. Specifically, research indicates that the cognitive benefits of aerobic exercise like Tensegrity exceed those of ordinary aerobic exercise, due to the complex and bilateral nature of the movements, as well as the continuous learning opportunity presented by the large volume of Tensegrity series.

Reducing Attachments

The enhancement of perceptual abilities, such as memory, attention and executive function, is only one step toward expanding awareness and enabling it to shift into a realm of new possibilities. In order to utilize enhanced perception, the fixation of perception to daily affairs must be broken. Otherwise, as long as perception is exclusively devoted to day-to-day concerns, there is no possibility of perceiving anything beyond the ordinary world. In other words, perception must acquire some degree of fluidity and freedom, in order to move away from its attachment to daily life.

Our day-to-day energies and activities are primarily dedicated to the things that we believe have importance, value and interest, such as ourselves, our friends and family, our possessions, and our worldly aspirations. Indeed, our "self" is highly integrated with the daily world and supremely important. Therefore, freedom from the daily world particularly includes letting go of the "self".

In addition, cultural and social environments demand adherence to both explicit and implicit rules and regulations (e.g. being successful at work, paying bills, following the law, etc.). As a consequence, stress, anxiety, worry and concern act to keep perception fixated on those things we deem important and valuable. Conversely, reductions in stress, anxiety, worry and concern can help to free awareness from the habits, routines and preoccupations of daily life.

For example, one prevalent source of stress and anxiety, even in normal populations, is self-presentation (18). Other forms of stress and anxiety originate from time pressure, workload (19), job demands, interpersonal relations and social responsibilities as well as any perception of potentially harmful situations (18). Self-image is one of those things that we deem to be very important, since it can determine cost/reward in various social situations such as work and school, or with family and friends. Consequently, the stress and anxiety associated with upholding and defending a self-image results in a significant dedication and expenditure of energy, creating a fixation on the self.

Because a great deal of awareness and energy is dedicated to projecting and defending a self-image, Castaneda (20 p. 37) asserts that losing self-importance, or at least dethroning it, is a critical component of shamanic practice. Consequently, significant perceptual resources, including memory, attention and volition, can be freed from protecting and maintaining the desired self-image.

Unfortunately, self-presentation, and daily life in general, produce stress and anxiety that can have adverse effects on perceptual abilities like executive function. Specifically, *attentional inhibition* and *attentional shifting* are diminished, intensifying the fixation of perception on the daily world. In other words, anxiety can increase the fixation of attention to daily concerns, and reduce an individual's ability to control their own attention (21).

Memory and attention can also suffer performance issues as a result of stress (19), and because memory, attention and executive function are fundamental process-abilities of perception, diminished performance in these process-abilities effectively limits perception.

Castaneda (1 p. 3) writes about perceptual limitations in similar terms, declaring that we are restricted to the boundaries of *normal* perception because all of our energy is devoted to behaviors established by our cultural and social environment.

Tart (22 p. 64) reiterates how cultural and social demands can psychologically dominate and stabilize individual awareness by fully engaging an individual's perceptual resources. Tart describes the consistent dedication of cognitive resources toward daily activities as a 'psychological loading' mechanism that consumes so much perceptual energy that very little is left over for perceiving non-ordinary reality.

Of particular relevance, Tart (22 pp. 71-72) suggests that induction of a discrete-Altered State of Consciousness (d-ASC) is facilitated by disrupting the processes that stabilize the baseline-State Of Consciousness (b-SOC), citing drugs and exercise as two methods of induction. However, it is important to note that despite writing about psychedelic drugs, Castaneda never advocated drug use, but instead prescribed the use of shamanic practices to reach non-ordinary states of reality.

In essence, if an individual's energy is principally dedicated to the desired activities of daily life and defending the self-image, as well as fulfilling cultural and social demands of the daily world, then perception is restricted to the bounds of *ordinary daily awareness*, and not free to experience possibilities that lie beyond those boundaries. In other words, if our physical and cognitive energies, including memory, attention and volition, are consistently devoted to the concerns of our day-to-day life, then how can we expect to perceive anything beyond our day-to-day life?

Underhill (23 p. 51) offers a sobering perspective on this subject, as she squarely hits the mark in describing how deeply invested we are in our daily lives. Consequently, her words illuminate *how freeing perception from the constraints that limit awareness* is an important undertaking in conjunction with *enhancing perceptual abilities.* In other words, what good is enhancing perception, if it remains "harnessed to the wrong machine"?

> It is not merely that your intellect has assimilated, united with a superficial and unreal view of the world. Far worse: your will, your desire, the sum total of your energy, has been turned the wrong way, harnessed to the wrong machine. You have become accustomed to the idea that you want, or ought to want, certain valueless things, certain specific positions ... and thither your heart perpetually tends to stray. Habit has you in its chains. You are not free.

Tart (22 pp. 64-67) echoes the same sentiment, although in a more analytic fashion, when he details four major ways that our awareness is made resistant to change (stabilized), enabling it to maintain allegiance to ordinary daily activities and thereby preventing experiences of non-ordinary reality.

> Loading Stabilization - Loading in general refers to any activity that draws a large proportion of the energy of the system so that the system does not have excess free energy available.
>
> Negative Feedback Stabilization - Negative feedback refers to a correction process initiated when a structure or system starts to go or has gone beyond acceptable limits, and is designed to decrease undesirable deviation.
>
> Positive Feedback Stabilization - Positive feedback refers to an active reward process that occurs when a structure or subsystem is functioning within acceptable limits and that strengthens functioning within those limits.
>
> Limiting Stabilization - limiting stabilization, consists of interfering with the ability of some subsystems or structures to function in a way that might destabilize the ongoing state of consciousness. It limits the functional range of certain subsystems.

There is an abundance of examples that illustrate the various stabilization processes operating around us and how they harness awareness/energy to the machinery of society. Loading stabilization is evident in the busy lives we lead, while trying to meet the demands of our jobs and personal lives. How many times have you heard a phrase like, 'There aren't enough hours in the day to get everything done that needs to be done'? Negative feedback stabilization is also employed by societies, through structures such as crime and punishment, as well as social and peer pressure. Additionally, positive feedback is apparent in the rewards granted by a culture or society such as personal freedoms, monetary and material rewards, as well as recognition and fame. And finally, limiting stabilizations are evident in many forms, from laws that make psychedelic drugs illegal, to the deleterious effects that anxiety and stress impose on perception. Indeed, many of these processes operate concurrently, or in conjunction with each other, stabilizing and fixating our ordinary state of awareness and keeping it anchored to the patterns and routines of our daily lives.

Therefore, the second part of our hypothesis claims the *Magical Passes*, in the generic form of Tensegrity, are one of the practices that further enable the enhancement of perception and the expansion of awareness by reducing attachments to the patterns and routines associated with ordinary daily awareness. In support of this premise, we again turn to the literature on aerobic exercise, focusing on the benefits of exercise that reduce attachments and decrease the fixation of perception.

To begin with, it is a well-established fact that stress and anxiety have significant detrimental effects on cognition and perception. Staal (19) provides a thorough and comprehensive literature review of the effects of various stressors on cognition. While Staal concedes that a unified definition of stress is lacking in the scientific community, he adopts a definition that reveals the subtle presence of stress in day-to-day activities, as individuals attempt to cope with the demands placed on them by work, family and society.

> [Stress is] the interaction between three elements: perceived demand, perceived ability to cope, and the perception of the importance of being able to cope with the demand.

Stress, anxiety, worry and concern are common, even among individuals without clinically diagnosed anxiety disorders (24). In fact, social anxiety is a widespread phenomenon in normal populations and, as previously mentioned, self-presentation is a prevalent source of stress and anxiety (18).

In a thorough review of stress, Staal (19) examines a wide range of stressors including, workload, time pressure, thermal stress (heat and cold), noise and fatigue, as well as moderating factors like "social facilitation" and "social impairment". His review also discusses the effects of stress on processes that are key to perception, such as memory, attention, and executive functions like judgment and decision making.

Specifically, Staal (19) reviewed over thirty different studies that consistently showed negative effects of stress and anxiety on memory. Some studies suggest memory is a resource that is made 'less available' by stressors.

Additionally, Staal (19) describes how negative effects on memory can cause individuals to resort to habitual, or over-learned, behaviors, thus keeping energy and awareness anchored to the habits, patterns and routines associated with ordinary daily activities.

> Tasks that are well-learned tend to be more resistant to the effects of stress than those that are less well-learned. Furthermore, when tasks are practiced and well-learned, they are likely to be committed to long-term memory, and through their frequent use (activation, rehearsal, and recollection) more easily remembered. Several authors have demonstrated that this kind of practice leads to automaticity and the proceduralization of tasks. Thus, these over-learned behaviors tend to require less attentional control and fewer mental resources, which further results in enhanced performance and greater resistance to stress. It is generally accepted that under stress, individuals tend to revert back to earlier well-learned responses.

Furthermore, when Staal (19) reviewed sixteen different studies examining the effects of stress on attention, including sustained attention and vigilance, he concluded that psychological stress narrows attention, creating a phenomenon known as "tunneling". Attentional tunneling is defined by Wickens (25) as "the allocation of attention to a particular channel of information, diagnostic hypothesis, or task goal, for a duration that is longer than optimal, given the expected cost of neglecting events on other channels ....". Consequently, stress, resulting from the demands of daily life, narrows attention, keeping it focused on the concerns of daily life.

> The research literature concerning stress' effects on attentional processes is relatively clear. Psychological stress along with various forms of workload tend to tunnel attention, reducing focus on peripheral information and tasks and centralizing focus on main tasks.

Moreover, when Staal (19) reviewed over forty relevant studies concerning the effects of stress on the executive functions of judgment and decision making, he concluded that judgment and decision making are also degraded. Again, the research indicates that, "Individuals tend to rely on [well-learned] responses regardless of their previous response success".

> The research literature concerning the effects of stress on judgment and decision making demonstrates that both individual and team processes are degraded. ... As fewer alternatives are considered, there is a recursion to previously sampled possibilities. Individuals tend to rely on these previous responses regardless of their previous response success. Thus, in addition to experiencing greater rigidity, individuals may tend to persist with a method or strategy even after it has ceased to be helpful. This assumes that the previous strategy or approach is well-learned.

The research also indicates that individuals, as well as groups, may adopt "load shedding" as a coping strategy, to simplify tasks, thereby inhibiting "...non-essential information from being processed."

In other words, as cognitive resources are deployed to their capacity, information that is deemed "non-essential", gets ignored. Castaneda (26 p. 88) summarily expresses the consequences of loading perception to capacity with daily affairs. Possibilities that exist outside of ordinary reality are deemed non-essential and superfluous. In the end, there is too little awareness/energy left over for anything beyond ordinary daily awareness.

> "The unknown is forever present," he continued, "but it is outside the possibility of our normal awareness. The unknown is the superfluous part of the average man. And it is superfluous because the average man doesn't have enough free energy to grasp it."

According to the *stabilization* analysis proposed by Tart (22 pp. 63-69), these deleterious effects that stress and anxiety impose on memory, attention and executive function, are a type of *limiting stabilization*, since diminished cognitive performance results in limited perceptual ability.

However, even though numerous empirical studies conclude that stress and anxiety can limit perception by; diminishing memory performance, narrowing the scope of attention and discouraging intentional behavior by creating habitual reliance on well-learned routines, Tensegrity, when consistently practiced, can counteract these limitations in a number of ways.

For example, consistent Tensegrity practice requires the practitioner to redeploy some amount of time and energy (physical and cognitive) away from ordinary daily activities and toward practicing the movements. As a result, the practitioner is distracted, at least temporarily, from the usual stressors associated with ordinary daily life. Specifically, both *exercise* and *cognitive based distractions*, have been studied and found to be equally effective at reducing state anxiety, but exercise was found more effective at reducing trait anxiety (27). According to Tart's stabilization analysis, withdrawing energy from ordinary daily activities can facilitate the possibility of disrupting the ordinary state of consciousness by interfering with the loading stabilization that keeps "a person's consciousness busy with desired types of activities". Stefan (28) decisively concluded that learning motor sequences requires the use of attentional resources. Therefore, when attention is directed toward learning Tensegrity sequences, it is effectively diverted away from daily concerns.

Tensegrity also disrupts habitual reliance on well-learned routines, by temporarily halting over-learned routines, forcing the practitioner to intentionally engage memory, attention and executive function, rather than rely on habitual behaviors. According to Castaneda (29 pp. 74-75), *disrupting the routines of life*, is an important shamanic practice. Castaneda's teacher used hunting to point out that Castaneda, like the game he was hunting, was also caught in a series of routines, habits and patterns that he needed to disrupt in order to free himself from the fixation of those routines.

Tensegrity also reduces stress and anxiety, and the resultant narrowing of attention, through the physiological interaction of muscular tension and relaxation. As previously noted, Castaneda (1 p. 36) tells us that Tensegrity "is in essence the interplay between relaxing and tensing the muscles of choice parts of the body ". And according to the work conducted by Dr Edmund Jacobson more than fifty years ago, which is still valid today, there is medical and psychological significance in muscular states. Jacobson (30 p. xvi) determined that psychological states and muscular states are intimately connected. It is perhaps the connection between muscular states and mental states that underlies the shamanic idea that body positions and movements affect perception, or in Castaneda's terms, the *Magical Passes* can move the assemblage point.

Jacobson (30) ultimately developed a technique for achieving a state of deep relaxation, by first tensing a muscle for a few seconds and then relaxing it. The progressive tensing and relaxing of various muscle groups, throughout the body, was found to induce both a physical and psychological state of calm relaxation and particularly the relaxation of "mental activities" (30 pp. 431, 188).

> I have offered evidence that proprioceptive sensations from muscular contractions are important elements in the "stream of consciousness"; that as these diminish with advancing relaxation, not alone kinesthetic but also visual and auditory images become fewer, until for recurrent brief periods, at least, mental activity is so to speak shut off.

***

> Motor or kinesthetic imagery likewise may be relaxed away. "Inner speech," for instance, ceases with progressive relaxation of the muscles of the lips, tongue, larynx and throat.

Castaneda (26 pp. 136-137) used the phrase "internal dialogue" as opposed to Jacobson's "inner speech", and regarded shutting off inner speech, or stopping the internal dialogue, as an important and significant shamanic accomplishment. Castaneda also referred to stopping the internal dialogue as *inner silence.* According to Castaneda (1 p. 24), the *Magical Passes* result in the "redeployment of energy, and its three concomitants-the shutting off of internal dialogue, the possibility for inner silence, and the fluidity of the assemblage point."

Because the fundamental nature of Tensegrity is to tense and relax various muscles throughout the body, practitioners are presented with an opportunity to develop a heightened sensitivity to tension and relaxation. In fact, many of the components of Tensegrity, such as muscle relaxation, breath training and physical exercise are all cited in the literature as stress management methods (31 pp. 59-60).

> Relaxation of the skeletal muscle controls, produces a state of rest throughout the neuromuscular circuits, including reduced activity of the brain itself.

Indeed, Progressive Muscle Relaxation (PMR) techniques have been shown to turn off the stress response and elicit a general relaxation response. Consequently, many of the adverse physical and mental effects caused by chronic stress can be reduced or even eliminated through regular practice (32).

The physical and psychological state of calm relaxation produced through tensing and relaxing muscles, can provide the practitioner with a respite from the expectations, demands, anxieties and stressors of the daily world. As practice progresses, individuals can better discern states of tension and relaxation, even using Tensegrity to achieve an enhanced state of well-being. A state of calm relaxation and a sense of well-being, can reduce the practitioner's level of concern and worry regarding daily affairs. Many individuals seek respite from their daily concerns through various forms of relaxation, including the use of drugs and alcohol, which unlike exercise, can be harmful to cognitive function.

Tensegrity reduces attachments to the patterns and routines of daily awareness by counteracting the deleterious effects that stress and anxiety have on perception. As previously discussed, stress and anxiety impose significant limitations on perception, creating a sort of perceptual rigidity, by impairing memory, diminishing attentional control, narrowing the range of attention, degrading judgment and decision making, and increasing reliance on established routines. However, research has consistently shown that physical exercise, like Tensegrity, can not only reduce stress and anxiety but also increase resilience to stress, thereby decreasing or even eliminating the perceptual limitations imposed by stress and anxiety.

For example, Conn (24) conducted a meta-analysis of studies that investigated anxiety outcomes for healthy adults, without anxiety disorders, when they increased their physical activity. Conn (24) defined anxiety as "a mental state or feeling of uneasiness, apprehension, tension, fear, worry, and/or concern". The results of the nineteen eligible reports indicated that physical activity reduced anxiety in the healthy subjects.

Petruzzello (27) conducted three separate meta-analyses, using more than one hundred different studies on the anxiety reducing effects of exercise. The investigators concluded that aerobic exercise, of at least twenty-one minutes, resulted in reducing both state and trait anxiety.

Some studies (33) (34) show that exercise is just as effective as anti-depressive medications in treating depression, while other studies (35) (34) (36) (37) indicate that exercise "confers enduring resilience to stress."

These relevant studies clearly show that physical exercises, such as Tensegrity practice, counteract stress and anxiety, consequently acting to diminish the deleterious effects they inflict on the perceptual process-abilities of memory, attention and volition. Therefore, Tensegrity presents itself as a method to free perception from the bonds of *daily awareness* by counteracting the narrowing and fixation of perception caused by anxiety and stress. Indeed, Tensegrity can be seen not only as an opportunity to improve perceptual abilities, but also as an opportunity to reduce the attachment of perception to the *daily world*; by recovering attentional control from the worry and concern of daily affairs, by expanding memory and attention beyond the narrowed limits of day-to-day life, and by breaking the chains of habit and routine that bind awareness to the daily world. As long as perception remains dedicated to the concerns of ordinary reality, it is like the tethered goat, and "Where the goat is tethered, there it must browse."

Furthermore, because of its ability to reduce the effects of stress and anxiety, as well as produce resilience to stress, Tensegrity can be an important tool for practitioners who pursue excursions into non-ordinary reality, since those excursions may themselves be quite stressful. Crews (38) performed a meta-analytic review of thirty-four studies that examined the effects of aerobic fitness on resistance to psychosocial stressors, and concluded that "… aerobically fit subjects had a reduced psychosocial stress response compared to either control group or baseline values." Castaneda (1 pp. 3, 4) openly acknowledges the necessity of physical fitness, for travelers who venture into the unknown.

Moreover, some studies (4) (39) (36) (40) go beyond associating exercise with only anxiety reducing effects and stress resilience, and declare that exercise actually enhances psychological well-being.

> Exercise is associated with a reduction in physiological measures of stress and psychological measures such as anxiety and depression. Further, exercise is associated with elevations in mood states and heightened psychological well-being
>
> ***
>
> Physical activity appears to relieve symptoms of depression and anxiety and improve mood. … Physical activity appears to improve health-related quality of life by enhancing psychological well-being and by improving physical functioning in persons compromised by poor health.
>
> ***
>
> Together, this body of research suggests that moderate regular exercise should be considered as a viable means of treating depression and anxiety and improving mental well-being in the general public.
>
> ***
>
> The results indicate a consistent association between enhanced psychological well-being, measured using a variety of psychological inventories, and regular physical exercise.

Castaneda (1 p. 15) also attributed a sensation of well-being to Tensegrity practice.

The numerous scientific studies cited above, confirm that stress and anxiety degrade perceptual performance by "tunneling attention" and "reducing focus on peripheral information", by "impairing elements of working memory" and increasing reliance "on [well-learned] responses, regardless of their previous response success", by degrading judgment and decision making, and by "decreasing attentional control", specifically, attentional inhibition and attentional shifting. Each of these impairments acts in a manner to narrow the range of perception and keep it fixated on the daily world, and therefore constrained within the boundaries of everyday life.

In addition, studies show that stress and anxiety are common, even among individuals without clinically diagnosed anxiety disorders. In fact, sources of stress and anxiety are quite diverse, ever-present and widespread even in normal populations. Sources of stress include, self-presentation, time pressure, workload, job demands, interpersonal relations, social responsibilities and essentially any situation deemed important, where perceived demand exceeds the perceived ability to cope.

The various studies and meta-analyses cited above, confirm the ability of aerobic exercise, like Tensegrity, to reduces stress and anxiety, thereby mitigating the aforementioned detrimental effects that stress and anxiety impose on perceptual process-abilities. Note also that the anxiety reducing effects of exercise are independent of age and health status. In other words, even healthy subjects experience anxiety reduction following physical exercise.

Consequently, a dedication to learning and practicing Tensegrity can provide regular distraction from the normal stressors of everyday life by diverting memory attention and volition away from ordinary daily activities. In addition, it can incorporate an assortment of novel behavior into daily life. It can also elicit mental relaxation through alternate muscular tension and relaxation, and foster psychological well-being, which reduces the stress and anxiety that keep perception fixated on ordinary daily affairs.

Taken together, the various studies cited above support the second part of our hypothesis which claims Tensegrity is one of the practices that can further enable the enhancement of perception and the expansion of awareness by reducing attachments to the patterns and routines associated with ordinary daily awareness. Because Tensegrity is a form of aerobic exercise that incorporates various relaxation techniques, such as specific breathing forms and muscular tension/relaxation, it reduces stress and anxiety as well as the accompanying perceptual impairments that keep perception limited and continually fixated on the patterns and routines of daily awareness. Specifically, regular Tensegrity practice can; create an opportunity to choose intentional behavior by reducing the repetition and reliance on daily habits and routines; expand the scope of attention beyond daily concerns by improving attentional control and mitigating attentional tunneling; and even provide stress resilience when facing uncertainty or venturing into unknown territory. In essence, Tensegrity can liberate awareness from the tether of habits, routines and stressors that limit perception and keep awareness fixated primarily on the concerns of daily life.

Activating New Possibilities

The third part of our hypothesis asserts that *Magical Passes* are a practice that can activate new possibilities for perception that that lie beyond the boundaries of ordinary daily awareness. Here, the phrase, *new possibilities*, refers to opportunities for perception to organize, identify and interpret the *energy at large* in new ways. In other words, to see the world through new eyes, to become aware of things previously disregarded, to perceive the truly novel and even experience the unknown. Huxley (41 p. 9) captures the essence of *new possibilities*, describing them as "something more than, and above all something different from, the carefully selected utilitarian material which our narrowed, individual minds regard as a complete … picture of reality."

However, it is William Blake who most eloquently describes the perceptual situation of man.

> If the doors of perception were cleansed everything would appear to man as it is: Infinite.
> For man has closed himself up, till he sees all things through narrow chinks of his cavern.

Castaneda (1 p. 3) (42 p. vii) makes it clear that the ultimate goal of his training was to <u>break the parameters of normal perception</u> - to 'cleanse the doors of perception' in order to perceive "something more than, and above all something different from" ordinary reality.

And while there are a wide variety of chemical methods, such as alcohol, drugs, inhalants, etc., that can "by-pass the reducing valve" of *normal perception*, Abelar (42 p. xiii) cautions that the shaman's aim is for "a sober, pragmatic, new way of perceiving".

In reaching for *new possibilities*, shaman found the perception of the left-body/right hemisphere to be indispensable. Castaneda (1 pp. 139, 140) (43 p. 167) tells us that the shaman of ancient Mexico saw that human beings are "composed of two complete functioning bodies", and they used that fundamental division as an opportunity to effectively employ the left body/right hemisphere.

> Don Juan taught his disciples that for the shamans who lived in Mexico in ancient times, the concept that a human being is composed of two complete functioning bodies, one on the left and one on the right, was fundamental to their endeavors ...

As previously discussed, McGilchrist (44 pp. 43, 27, 220) asserts fundamental differences between the two hemispheres in perceptual abilities, such as memory, attention and volition. Specifically, the right hemisphere has longer working memory and access to more information as well as a form of attention that is broad and vigilant.

Without doubt, the left body/right hemisphere, has essential characteristics that can facilitate *new possibilities*. Specifically, attention in the left-body/right hemisphere is "broad, open, and directed towards whatever else is going on in the world apart from ourselves" (44 p. 27). In addition, "virtually all the qualities listed by Walter Cannon as the hallmarks of the creative mind are features of right hemisphere function" (44 p. 468 n85). Indeed, the results of a meta-analysis (45) examining the lateralization of creativity "… suggest relative dominance of the right hemisphere during creative thinking." Furthermore, the right hemisphere plays "a large part, and in most cases the principal part," in imagination and creativity (44 p. 127). And, "It is the RH that is attuned to the apprehension of anything new" (44 p. 40). Furthermore, "The attentional system that detects stimuli outside the focus of conscious processing, is strongly lateralized to the right hemisphere" (44 p. 187). Moreover, the left body/right hemisphere is also the "silent" hemisphere, providing a fertile environment for *new possibilities*; an arena for perception to be free from the constraints of verbal language, its structure and syntax. In summary, the left body/right hemisphere possesses characteristics that promote opportunities for perception to organize, identify and interpret the energy at large in new ways.

Therefore, the third part of our hypothesis claims, the *Magical Passes*, in the generic form of Tensegrity, are one of the practices that further enable the enhancement of perception and the expansion of awareness by activating new possibilities for perception that lie beyond the boundaries of *ordinary daily awareness*. In support of this premise, we cite a variety of scientific studies that highlight the extraordinary and unique ways that Tensegrity stimulates the left body/right hemisphere, thereby opening perception to *new possibilities*.

To begin with, Tensegrity is conducted in an atmosphere with minimal left hemisphere stimulation and hence, more favorable to right hemisphere activation. In other words, an environment that diminishes perceptual loading on the left hemisphere. Indeed, Castaneda (1 p. 25) recommends that Tensegrity practice should be detached from the *concerns of our daily world* and performed in an environment free from *dialogue* and *other familiar elements*. Each of these items; *dialogue* and *familiar elements* as well as the *concerns of our daily world* (particularly planning and manipulation) predominantly activate the left hemisphere (44 pp. 464 n17, 40, 114). Therefore, minimizing or eliminating these items from the practice environment, diminishes left hemisphere stimulation, consequently creating an atmosphere more conducive to right hemisphere activation.

While immersed in an atmosphere conducive to the right hemisphere, Tensegrity also employs unusual or novel behavior, which has been shown to increase activity in the right hemisphere, because it not only presents an opportunity to learn new skills, but it also engages the body in unusual ways of breathing and moving. McGilchrist (44 p. 40) compares the right and left hemispheres, citing various scientific studies that indicate right hemisphere activation and/or involvement, more than left hemisphere, during novel experiences. Specifically, right hemispheric *attention* and *memory* (via the hippocampus) are engaged in novel experiences.

McGilchrist (44 p. 113) also notes that portions of the right hemisphere are activated whenever exploratory, versus grasping, motions are made regardless of which hand is used. This case is particularly relevant to Tensegrity movements that use the hands to sense or explore energy surrounding the body. Indeed, McGilchrist (44 p. 66) asserts that both hands stimulate the right hemisphere because it is the right hemisphere that maintains a *whole-body image*, while the left hemisphere maintains only a *right body image.*

Supporting evidence for right hemisphere activation, caused by bodily movement, is provided by Naito (15), where the investigators concluded that there is a right hemispheric dominance in kinesthetic processing, regardless of whether the left or right body is stimulated. Consequently, the kinesthetic nature of Tensegrity practice increases activity in right hemisphere brain areas, since it involves the kinesthetic sensations of muscles, tendons, and joints.

> Furthermore, our results provide evidence for a right hemisphere dominance for perception of limb movement.

McGilchrist (44 p. 69) explains that the right hemisphere has superior proprioceptive awareness, confirming that the various bodily movements of Tensegrity do indeed preferentially stimulate the right hemisphere.

In addition, several studies (46) (47) have concluded that postural balance is mainly controlled by the right hemisphere. These studies have drawn their conclusions by comparing control groups and subjects with right versus left hemisphere strokes or lesions. In fact, one study indicated that "A widespread network, mainly sitting in the right hemisphere, subserves this postural system." Consequently, the numerous Tensegrity movements that involve postural balance, are undoubtedly activating that "widespread network, mainly sitting in the right hemisphere".

Furthermore, Tensegrity increases activity in the right hemisphere, by specifically engaging the left body in two ways. First, according to Castaneda, "the most crucial element in the training of the shamans of ancient Mexico" is a group of Tensegrity movements, called the Heat Series, that requires motions in the left body only, while holding the right body immobile (1 p. 143). Movement sequences that are exclusive to the left body, strongly activate motor and proprioceptive regions of the right hemisphere, while eliciting minimal left hemisphere activity. It is telling that Castaneda declares the Heat Series as the most crucial element in shamanic training since this series of movements clearly gives preference to the right hemisphere/left body.

Indeed, Goldstein (48) concluded that not only do left body movements activate the right hemisphere, but they also produce a corresponding enhancement in creativity – a right brain attribute. Their investigation showed that left body movements, specifically contractions of the left hand, predominantly activate the right hemisphere, enabling perception to expand into an arena of creative thought.

Similarly, Propper (49) found that hand clenching increases neuronal activity in the contralateral hemisphere, and can therefore be used to activate and investigate functional specializations of the hemispheres.

Tensegrity also engages the left body in a second way that increases activity in the right hemisphere. Specifically, as a rule, every Magical Pass movement, regardless of the series, begins with the left body (1 p. 30) and then it is repeated with the right body. This order of precedence initiates activity in the right hemisphere first, followed by activity in both hemispheres when the movement is repeated on the right side. Even though the left hemisphere is activated when the right body is moved, the right hemisphere remains dominant for the perception of limb movement (15). Preferentially activating the left body first, and placing it in an "activated first", more dominant perceptual position, is reminiscent of Castaneda's (50 p. 259) 'dreaming' experience, which resulted in merging the "right and left awareness into one in which the order of predominance has been switched and the left has gained supremacy."

Moreover, Tensegrity may foster innovative perspectives, and novel perceptions, due to the variety of non-ordinary motor movements that activate specific neuronal groups in differing sequences, particularly the activation of the left body first. Because "neurons that fire together, wire together", new connections can be made in the nervous system. New neural connections can be created and reinforced by repeating novel movement sequences that associate various neuronal groups through progressive activation. The type of novel activity offered by Tensegrity is counter to the usual behaviors and sequences that are endlessly repeated day after day. The continual repetition of habitual behaviors and movements does not create new connections and instead reinforces existing neural connections, effectively limiting neuronal activity to a reduced operational space within the neural network. On the other hand, the atypical movements and novel behaviors, accomplished during Tensegrity practice, can expand activity within the neural network, and its possibilities, by creating new connections and reducing the reinforcement of habitual behaviors and movements.

And finally, Tensegrity appears to employ movement, metaphor and gesture as teaching tools directed at the right hemisphere, specifically, through a process that Madan and Singhal (51) have called "embodied cognition". The idea of "embodied cognition" suggests that "motor systems play an important role in cognition", emphasizing the importance of movement and gesture in memory. In other words, the body influences the mind and can even reinforce ideas that are performed in parallel with movement.

According to the idea of embodied cognition (51) then, Tensegrity phrases such as; *gathering energy*, *getting the assemblage point loose*, *hurling the assemblage point*, *legs rule vitality*, *the recapitulation window*, and *the center for decisions*, are more likely to be retained in memory when accompanied by their respective movements. It's worth repeating that Embodied Cognition "suggests that motor output is integral to cognition, and the converging evidence of multiple avenues of research further indicate that the role of our body in memory processes may be much more prevalent than previously believed."

In addition, the <u>metaphorical</u> nature of the phrases used in Tensegrity, specifically target the right hemisphere (52) (44 pp. 51, 71, 115). Phrases such as *calling of intent*, *energy as a wind-like vibration*, the *human form* system of interpretation, as well as the evolution of awareness called *total freedom*, are best understood by the right hemisphere, since it is particularly attuned to metaphor.

Furthermore, Tensegrity is not just movement, but <u>enactment</u> - gestures with meaning. Again, the right hemisphere is the locus of interpretation for metaphor and gestures (44 p. 59), like grinding, mixing, stirring and gathering energy (1 pp. 42-43,120,125). Indeed, the enacted movements along with the symbolic names that Castaneda (1 p. 125) assigned to various Tensegrity movements, appear to be suggestive aids to not only enlist the right hemisphere, but also guide the practitioner's memory, attention and intent, to help produce the desired effect.

> Something in the intent of hurling the assemblage point causes a profound effect toward the actual displacement of it.

McGilchrist (44 p. 228) summarizes the condition of left hemisphere dominance that Tensegrity attempts to offset as a perceptual world dominated by language, logic and linearity. A world that is the essence of our conscious experience.

In light of the foregoing evidence, Tensegrity practice can be seen as a systematic approach, that uses various elements, to stimulate the left body/right hemisphere and encourage activation of underutilized perceptual resources. These resources are key to activating new possibilities for perception that lie beyond the boundaries of *ordinary daily awareness* and include enhanced creativity (48) (45), generating novel associations (53) (44 pp. 33,42,94), and divergent thinking (53), as well as broad and open attention (44 pp. 27,43). Ultimately, activation of the right hemisphere supports and promotes *new possibilities*, such as seeing the world through new eyes, becoming aware of things previously disregarded, making disparate connections, being sensitive to subtleties, ultimately supporting the ability of the right hemisphere to free us from the hall of mirrors created by the left hemisphere.

Our primary focus throughout this chapter has been on the cognitive and perceptual enhancements that Tensegrity can foster in the practitioner. But, before concluding our review of Tensegrity, it is important to briefly discuss the idea put forth by Castaneda (1 p. 4) that Tensegrity is the first step toward the *redeployment of energy*. Clearly, the idea of *redeploying energy* applies to the cognitive facilities and psychical energies discussed throughout this book. But physical energy and the physical body are also very important because the body is the physical substrate for material energy to be converted, absorbed and made available for perception. As Castaneda (50 p. 163) points out, "…all the faculties, possibilities, and accomplishments of [shamanism], from the simplest to the most astounding, are in the human body itself." Therefore, it is significant that Castaneda (1 p. 15) identifies "centers of vitality", which he specifies as areas of the liver, gallbladder, pancreas, spleen and kidneys. Interestingly, each of these areas correspond to a gland or an organ that is vitally important for energy management in the human body. Specifically, the liver, gallbladder, pancreas, spleen and kidneys play a primary role in generating physical and cognitive energy from digestion and managing energy metabolism.

Fundamentally, all the cells of the body primarily derive energy from glucose and oxygen gathered from digestion and respiration. Glucose and oxygen are transported throughout the body by blood moving through the circulatory system. Physical activities, like Tensegrity, are known to produce an increase in blood flow, improve oxygenation of the body, massage internal organs, strengthen the immune system, develop cardiorespiratory endurance, increase muscular strength and improve balance. Regular physical activity makes the body healthier, stronger, more resilient, and more energy efficient. According to the Surgeon General's Report (39), regular aerobic exercise; "improves the efficiency of the aerobic energy-producing systems", "has been shown to bolster the function of certain components of the human immune system", and "may help prevent falls by improving muscle strength, functional capacity, gait, balance, and reaction time". The report also concludes that, "Physical activity reduces the risk of premature mortality in general, and of coronary heart disease, hypertension, colon cancer, and diabetes mellitus in particular. Physical activity also improves mental health and is important for the health of muscles, bones, and joints". In summary, "The body responds to physical activity in ways that have important positive effects on musculoskeletal, cardiovascular, respiratory, and endocrine systems."

The cardiovascular and respiratory systems are the essential energy delivery systems for every cell in the body; supplying the musculoskeletal system with the energy needed to support movement, and supplying the central nervous system with the energy necessary for cognitive function. Indeed, the brain appears to be fundamental to any enhancement of perception and its supply of biochemical energy is vital to its proper function. Interestingly, the brain represents only about 2% of body weight, and yet it accounts for nearly 20% of the caloric energy consumed by the body. Clearly, the brain - representing a central element in cognition - has tremendous energy requirements, that are best supported by a healthy body.

Therefore, the physical benefits of Tensegrity are an important component in <u>maintaining a healthy body and an efficient energy system</u>, as well as supporting the enhancement of cognitive abilities. Cotman (54), summarizes the cascade of cognitive benefits that result from exercise.

> Exercise sets into motion an interactive cascade of growth factor signaling that has the net effect of stimulating plasticity, enhancing cognitive function, attenuating the mechanisms driving depression, stimulating neurogenesis and improving cerebrovascular perfusion.

Indeed, Gomez-Pinilla (6) points to important exercise-induced changes in the body, at the molecular and genetic levels, that act to enhance cognitive abilities.

> ...exercise activates the neural circuitry important for learning and memory using molecular systems associated with synaptic plasticity and energy metabolism.

***

> ...exercise has the capacity to influence epigenetic mechanisms that modulate cognitive abilities at the molecular level

In conclusion, the *Magical Passes*, and the generic form of Tensegrity, are one of the methods prescribed by Castaneda that employs a novel form of aerobic exercise to promote neurocognitive enhancements, stress reduction and activation of the right hemisphere, that synergistically combine to achieve the shaman's goal of enhancing perception and expanding awareness. Specifically, our literature search has uncovered abundant evidence that regular aerobic exercise, such as Tensegrity, can enhance perception by supporting improvements in memory, attention, executive function, and brain plasticity. Furthermore, evidence shows that exercise, like Tensegrity, is conducive to reducing stress and anxiety, as well as promoting stress resilience and feelings of well-being. Decreases in stress and anxiety encourage new ways of perceiving (perceptual fluidity), by not only freeing behavioral patterns from habits and routines, but also by freeing cognitive resources like attention, memory and executive function from the fixation of daily affairs. Moreover, we have presented evidence that Tensegrity practice specifically promotes activation of the right hemisphere, thereby opening a doorway into an arena of divergent thinking, creativity and new possibilities. In summary, we have presented evidence to support our hypothesis that the *Magical Passes*, and the generic form of Tensegrity, are one of the practices advocated by Castaneda that enhance perception and expand awareness; 1) by improving various cognitive processes associated with perception through training; 2) by reducing attachments to the patterns and routines of *ordinary daily awareness*; and 3) by activating new possibilities for perception that lie beyond the boundaries of *ordinary daily awareness*.

References

1. **Castaneda, Carlos.** *Magical Passes: The Practical Wisdom of the Shamans of Ancient Mexico.* New York, NY, USA : HarperCollins Publishers, Inc., 1998.

2. *Be smart, exercise your heart: exercise effects on brain and congition.* **Hillman, C. , et al.** New York, NY, USA : Nature Publishing Group, 2008, Nature Reviews Neuroscience, Vol. 9, pp. 58-65.

3. *Aerobic Exercise and Neurocognitive Performance: a Meta-Analytic Review of Randomized Control Trials.* **Smith, P, et al.** Philadelphia, PA, USA : Lippincott Williams & Wilkins, 2010, Psychosomatic Medicine, Vol. 72(3), pp. 239-252.

4. *Effects of acute bouts of exercise on cognition.* **Tomporowski, P.** Amsterdam, Netherlands : Elsevier, 2003, Acta Psychologica, Vol. 112, pp. 297-324.

5. *Cardiovascular fitness, cortical plasticity, and aging.* **Colcombe, S, et al.** Washington, DC, USA : US National Academy of Sciences, 2004, PNAS, Vol. 101(9), pp. 3316-3321.

6. *The Influence of Exercise on Cognitive Abilities.* **Gomez-Pinilla, F., Hillman, C.** Hoboken, New Jersey, USA : John WIley & Sons, 2013, Comprehensive Physiology, Vol. 3 (1), pp. 403-428.

7. *Acute coordinative exercise improves attentional performance in adolescents.* **Budde, H, et al.** Amsterdam, Netherlands : Elsevier, Neuroscience Letters, Vol. 441, pp. 219-223.

8. *Impairment in Shifting Attention in Autistic and Cerebellar Patients.* **Courchesne E, et al.** Washington DC, USA : American Psychological Association, Behavioral Neuroscience, Vol. 108(5), pp. 848-865.

9. **Castaneda, Carlos.** *Tales of Power.* New York, NY, USA : Touchstone / Simon & Schuster, 1974.

10. *Neurogenesis and Exercise: Past and Future Directions.* **van Praag, H.** Berlin, Germany : Springer, 2008, Neuromolecular Medicine, Vol. 10(2), pp. 128-140.

11. *Exercise Training Increases Size of Hippocampus and Improves Memory.* **Erickson, K, et al.** Washington DC, USA : US National Academy of Sciences, 2011, PNAS, Vol. 108(7), pp. 3017-3022.

12. *Neuroplasticity Promoted by Task Complexity.* **Carey J, et al.** Philadelphia, PA, USA : Lippincott Williams & Wilkins, 2005, Exercise and Sport Sciences Reviews, Vol. 33, pp. 24-31.

13. *Brain Damage, Behavior, Rehabilitation, Recovery, and Brain Plasticity.* **Jones, T, et al.** New York, NY, USA : John Wiley & Sons, 1998, Mental Retardation and Developmental Disabilities, Vol. 4, pp. 231-237.

14. *Effects of Physical Activity on Children's Executive Function: Contributions of Experimental Research on Aerobic Exercise.* **Best, J.** Amsterdam, Netherlands : Elsevier, 2010, Developmental Reviews, Vol. 30(4), pp. 331-551.

15. *Dominance of the Right Hemisphere and Role of Area 2 in Human Kinesthesia.* **Naito, E, et al.** Bethesda, MD, USA : American Physiological Society, 2005, Journal of Neurophysiology, Vol. 93, pp. 1020-1034.

16. *Acquiring "the Knowledge" of London's Layout Drives Structural Brain Changes.* **Woollett, K, Maguire E.** Cambridge, MA, USA : Cell Press, 2011, Current Biology, Vol. 21, pp. 2109-2114.

17. **Merzenich, M.** Exercise Makes Kids Smarter. *On The Brain.* [Online] 2007. http://www.onthebrain.com/2007/03/exercise-make-kids-smarter/.

18. *Social Anxiety and Self-Presentation: A Conceptualization and Model.* **Schlenker B, and Leary M.** Washington DC, USA : American Psychological Association, 1982, Psychological Bulletin, Vol. 92(3), pp. 641-669.

19. *Stress, Cognition, and Human Performance: A Literature Review and Conceptual Framework.* **Staal M.** Moffett Field, CA, USA : NASA STIPO, 2004, NASA Technical Memorandum - 2004-212824.

20. **Castaneda, Carlos.** *The Art of Dreaming.* New York, NY, USA : First HarperPerennial / HarperCollins Publishers, 1994.

21. *Anxiety and Cognitive Performance: Attentional Control Theory.* **Eysenck M, et al.** Washington DC, USA : American Psychological Association, 2007, Emotion, Vol. 7(2), pp. 336-353.

22. **Tart, C.** *States of Consciousness.* Lincoln, NE, USA : iUniverse.com Inc., 2000.

23. **Underhill, E.** *Practical Mysticism: A Little Book for Normal People.* New York, NY, USA : Vintage Spiritual Classics / Random House, 2003.

24. *Anxiety Outcomes After Physical Activity Interventions: Meta-Analysis Findings.* **Conn V.** Alphen aan den Rijn, Netherlands : Wolters Kluwer, 2010, Nursing Research , Vol. 59(3), pp. 224-231.

25. **Wickens C.** *Attentional Tunneling and Task Management.* AHFD, University of Illinois. Savoy, IL, USA : NASA, 2005.

26. **Castaneda, Carlos.** *The Fire from Within.* New York, NY, USA : Simon and Schuster, 1984.

27. *A Meta_Analysis on the Anxiety-Reducing Effects of Acute and Chronic Exercise: Outcomes and Mechanisms.* **Petruzzello S, et al.** New York, NY, USA : Springer International Publishing, 1991, Sports Medicine, Vol. 11(3), pp. 143-182.

28. *Modulation of Associative Human Motor Cortical Plasticity by Attention.* **Stefan K, et al.** Hoboken, NJ, USA : Wiley-Blackwell, Journal of Neurophysiology, Vol. 92(1), pp. 66-72.

29. **Castaneda C.** *Journey to Ixtlan: The Lessons of Don Juan.* New York, NY, USA : Washington Square Press, 1972.

30. **Jacobson E.** *Progressive Relaxation: A Physiological and Clinical Investigation of Muscular States and Their Significance in Psychology and Medical Practice.* Chicago, IL, USA : University of Chicago Press, 1938.

31. **Lehrer P.** *Principles and Practice of Stress Management 3rd Ed.* New York, NY, USA : Guilford Press, 2007.

32. *Effects of Progressive Relaxation and Classical Music on Measurements of Attention, Relaxation, and Stress Response.* **Scheufele P.** Berlin, Germany : Springer, 2000, Journal of Behavioral Medicine, Vol. 23(2), pp. 207-228.

33. *Exercise and Pharmacotherapy in the Treatment of Major Depressive Disorder.* **Blumenthal J.** Philadelphia, PA, USA : Lippincott Williams & Wilkins, 2007, Psychosomatic Medicine, Vol. 69(7), pp. 597-596.

34. *The Science of Resilience: Implications for the Prevention and Treatment of Depression.* **Southwick S, Charney D,.** Washington DC, USA : American Association for the Advancement of Science, 2012, Science, Vol. 338, pp. 79-82.

35. *Effects of Physical Exercise on Anxiety, Depression, and Sensitivity to Stress: A Unifying Theory.* **Salmon P.** Oxford, United Kingdom : Pergamon Press, 2001, Clinical Psychology Review, Vol. 21(1), pp. 33-61.

36. *The Influence of Physical Activity on Mental Well-Being.* **Fox K.** Cambridge, England : Cambridge University Press, 1999, Public Health Nutrition, Vol. 2(3a), pp. 411-418.

37. *Exercise, Stress Resistance, and Central Serotonergic Systems.* **Greenwood B.** Philadelphia, PA, USA : Lippincott Williams & Wilkins, 2011, Exercise and Sport Sciences Reviews, Vol. 39(3), pp. 140-149.

38. *A Meta-Analytic Review of Aerobic Fitness and Reactivity to Psychosocial Stressors.* **Crews D, Landers D,.** Philadelphia, PA, USA : Lippincott Williams & Wilkins, 1987, Medicine and Science in Sports & Exercise, Vol. 19, pp. 114-120.

39. **Manley A.** *Physical Activity and Health: A Report of the Surgeon General.* Washingto DC, USA : US Department of Health and Human Service, 1996.

40. *Physical Exercise and Psychological Well-Being: A Population Study in Finland.* **Hassmen P.** Amsterdam, Netherlands : Elsevier, 2000, Preventive Medicine, Vol. 30, pp. 17-25.

41. **Huxley A.** *The Doors of Percpetion.* New York, NY, USA : Harper & Row, 1954.

42. **Abelar, Taisha.** *The Sorcerers' Crossing: A Woman's Journey.* New York, NY, USA : Penguin Books USA Inc., 1992.

43. **Castaneda, Carlos.** *The Active Side of Infinity.* New York, NY, USA : HarperCollins Publishers, 1998.

44. **McGilchrist, Iain.** *The Master and his Emissary; The Divided Brain and the Makingof the Western World.* NewHaven, CT, USA : Yale University Press, 2010.

45. *Hemispheric Specialization and Creative Thinking: A Meta-Analytic Review of Lateralization of Creativity.* **Mihov K, et al.** Cambridge, MA, USA : Academic Press, 2010, Brain and Cognition, Vol. 72(3), pp. 442-448.

46. *Impairments of trunk movements following left orr ight hemisphere lesions: dissociation between apraxic errors and postural instability.* **Spinazzola L, et al.** Oxford, England : Oxford University Press, 2003, Brain, Vol. 126, pp. 2656-2666.

47. *Postural balance following stroke: towards a disadvantage of the right brain-damaged hemisphere.* **Pérennou D, et al.** Amsterdam, Netherlands : Elsevier, 1999, Revue Neurologique (Paris), Vol. 155(4), pp. 281-290.

48. *Unilateral Muscle Contractions Enhance Creative Thinking* . **Goldstein A, et al.** Madison, WI, USA : Psychonomic Society, 2010, Psychonomic Review & Bulletin, Vol. 17(6), pp. 895-899.

49. *Getting a Grip on Memory: Unilateral Hand Clenching Alters Episodic Recall.* **Propper, R., et al.** San Francisco, CA, USA : Public Library of Science, 2013, PLoS One, Vol. 8(4).

50. **Castaneda, Carlos.** *The Eagle's Gift.* New York, NY, USA : Pocket Books / Washinton Square Press / Simon & Schuster, 1981.

51. *Using actions to enhance memory :effects of enactment, gestures, and exercise on human memory.* **Madan C, Singhal A.** Lausanne, Switzerland : Frontiers Media, 2012, Frontiers in Psychology, Vol. 3(507).

52. *The role of the right hemisphere in the interpretation of figurative aspects of language A positron emission tomography activation study.* **Bottini G.** Oxford, England : Oxford University Press, 1994, Brain, Vol. 117, pp. 1241-1253.

53. *Enhanced divergent thinking and creativity in musicians: A behavioral and near-infrared spectroscopy study.* **Gibson C, et al.** Cambridge, MA, USA : Academic Press, 2009, Brain and Cognition, Vol. 69, pp. 162–169.

54. *Exercise builds brain health: key roles of growth factor cascades and inflammation.* **Cotman C, et al.** Cambridge, MA, USA : Cell Press, Trends in Neurosciences, Vol. 30(9), pp. 464-472.

CHAPTER 4

Recapitulation

****

Recapitulation, as described by Abelar (1 p. 46) and Castaneda (2 p. 148) (3 p. 106), is a lifelong practice that requires a systematic and detailed recollection of every event in our entire lives – "all the people we have met, all the places we have seen and all the feelings we have had". The recollection of each memory entails going further than simply recalling every possible detail, and instead, reliving the event, as if actually going into the memory, while simultaneously performing a natural, rhythmic breathing technique referred to as the "sweeping" or "cleansing" breath, which is used to "fan" or "sweep" the event. In some ways, Recapitulation is similar to a sitting meditation because it employs inward focus, visualization and concentration, as well as a particular breathing technique. However, Recapitulation differs in at least two significant ways from common forms of meditation. First, instead of focusing on the breath, an object, or mantra, the mental effort associated with Recapitulation involves the systematic retrieval of, and focus on, detailed episodic-autobiographical memories; working backward in time, "starting from the present, going back to the earliest memories". Second, a "fanning" or "sweeping" of the event, using the "cleansing" breath, requires coordinating inhalations and exhalations, with turning the head from side to side.

According to Castaneda and Abelar, Recapitulation has three essential components; a place of solitude, detailed recollections and the "cleansing" breath. The places of solitude described by Castaneda (4 pp. 284-288) and Abelar (1 pp. 57,240) include a custom built wooden crate, a snug cave and a tiny, one-room, tree house. These small, out of the way, places contribute important elements to the practice of Recapitulation, such as; separation from the daily world and its concerns, a place without disturbances to support long periods of concentration, and an environment with minimal distraction to aid in developing attentional focus and memory retrieval.

The recollection of each event involves reconstructing in one's mind, every possible detail, including all the physical details of the surroundings, the persons involved in the event, and even one's own feelings. The practitioner is advised to

"…enter into the locale itself, as if actually going into it", "to re-experience the events and feelings in as much detail as possible" and to relive, more than merely recollect.

The "cleansing" breath, used to "sweep" or "fan" the event, requires the practitioner to slowly and gently turn the head from side to side, while inhaling and exhaling. Specifically, the head is turned toward the right or left shoulder to start. A deep inhalation is taken as the head slowly turns toward the opposite shoulder. At that point, a deep exhalation begins as the head turns back to the starting position, where the exhalation ends. The inhalations and exhalations are synchronized with the turning of the head, and continue in a slow and rhythmic manner while the event is thoroughly recollected in one's mind.

Abelar (1 p. 57) provides some personal insight into the challenges associated with re-examining one's life, when she expresses her reluctance to dredge up the past and describes Recapitulation as "painstaking work". However, Underhill (5 p. 50) writes that, despite the difficulties associated with recollecting our life and our "self", the process can produce real change in those who practice it, and even put one's life in perspective with eternal values.

> Few can bear to contemplate themselves face to face; for the vision is strange and terrible, and brings awe and contrition in its wake. The life of the seer is changed by it forever. He is converted, in the deepest and most drastic sense; is forced to take up a new attitude towards himself and all other things. Likely enough, if you really knew yourself--saw your own dim character, perpetually at the mercy of its environment; your true motives, stripped for inspection and measured against eternal values; your unacknowledged self-indulgences; your irrational loves and hates--you would be compelled to remodel your whole existence, and become for the first time a practical man.

As previously mentioned, Castaneda recommended following the path of the shamans of ancient Mexico, so that a practitioner can systematically free their energy and redirect it toward shifting awareness into a new realm of possibilities. That shift in awareness, resulting from an enhancement of perception, is accomplished in the manner we have outlined as our hypothesis; 1) by improving various cognitive processes associated with perception through training; 2) by reducing attachments to the patterns and routines of *ordinary daily awareness*; and 3) by activating new possibilities for perception that lie beyond the boundaries of *ordinary daily awareness*.

Unfortunately, peer reviewed research on Recapitulation is completely lacking at this time, but we believe the practice shares many similarities with *Meditation* (*Focused Attention* and *Open Monitoring)*, *MEmory Specificity Training (MEST*), relaxation techniques such as *slow- paced diaphragmatic breathing* and *vagal stimulation*, as well as *memory reconsolidation* and *Hemispheric Retrieval/Encoding Asymmetry (HERA)*. Each of these areas, as well as others such as Prolonged Exposure Therapy, has peer reviewed literature that is relevant to an assessment of Recapitulation practice.

Focused Attention (FA) meditation is the practice of focusing and sustaining attention on something such as an object, a sound, a visualization, a sensation or the breath. FA meditation is different from Open Monitoring (OM) meditation which involves non-attachment and non-reactive monitoring of the moment-to-moment environment. Recapitulation can be viewed as a Focused Attention meditation that uses detailed episodic-autobiographical events as the object of attention. Recapitulation also shares qualities with Open Monitoring meditation since it promotes the development of non-attachment and non-reactive monitoring toward the autobiographical events that are more than recollected, but instead re-lived.

MEmory Specificity Training (MEST) is an instructional program that uses repeated memory retrieval practice to increase the specific nature of retrieved autobiographical memories. Participants are prompted to "recall as much (spatio-temporal, contextual, and sensory perceptual) details as possible" (6). Since Recapitulation is primarily involved with recalling episodic-autobiographical memories in as much detail as possible, the literature on this subject is particularly relevant because it indicates an improvement in recall with practice.

Slow-paced breathing, such as the "cleansing breath", goes by various names such as; deep breathing, diaphragmatic breathing and paced respiration. Slow-paced breathing entails slow, deep inhalations that expand the diaphragm and fill the lungs with oxygen, followed by slow, full exhalations that empty the lungs. The act of taking full breaths, in a slow rhythmic manner, increases oxygen exchange in the lungs, slows the heart rate, lowers blood pressure and increases relaxation. In addition, turning the head from side-to-side, during the "cleansing breath", stimulates the vagal nerves on either side of the neck, which also acts to slow heart rate and promote relaxation.

Memory reconsolidation, as described by Nader (7), is a term used for returning long-term (consolidated) memories to a volatile state, whenever they are recalled in sufficient detail. The recalled memory enters into a dynamic or fluid state, where it can be updated or changed before it undergoes a consolidation-like process again. In other words, there is a short time period after recalling a long-term memory, in sufficient detail, called the **reconsolidation window**. During the **reconsolidation window**, long term (consolidated) memories become volatile again, and are therefore receptive to change. Interestingly, Castaneda (3 p. 114) used the term "window of recapitulation", and Abelar (1 p. 46) described

Recapitulation as an opportunity to "expel foreign, undesirable energy that has accumulated in us."

We believe memory reconsolidation is a potentially powerful process that, when paired with relaxation techniques like slow-paced breathing and vagal stimulation, becomes the effective mechanism operating in Recapitulation practice. Specifically, recalling episodic-autobiographical memories returns the recollected memories to a dynamic state. In their volatile state, the memories recalled during Recapitulation are exposed to, and associated with, new information - a state of embodied physical relaxation that is induced by slow-paced breathing and vagal stimulation, before the memories are re-consolidated. In essence, the combination of solitude, safety, rhythmic breathing, and vagal stimulation elicit a state of calm relaxation that 'updates' the recollected memory with a feeling of 'calm-relaxation' and effectively 'cleanses' heavy emotions, hopes and fears associated with the recollected memory. Similar techniques, used in Prolonged Exposure Therapy, have proven successful in clinical cases of Post-Traumatic Stress Disorder (PTSD).

Hemispheric Encoding/Retrieval Asymmetry (HERA) is a model of memory encoding and retrieval that is based on a large set of experimental data. According to the model, the left hemisphere, specifically the left prefrontal cortex, is more involved in episodic memory *encoding,* while the right hemisphere, specifically the right prefrontal cortex, is more involved in episodic memory *retrieval*, hence the hemispheric asymmetry. Furthermore, right hemisphere brain regions are preferentially involved when memory recall includes emotional content and self-related processing. HERA research is therefore particularly relevant since stimulating the right hemisphere by recalling episodic memories – the act of Recapitulating – can activate right hemispheric characteristics that support new perceptual possibilities.

Therefore, the scientific literature on MEmory Specificity Training, Focused Attention meditation, Open Monitoring meditation, slow-paced breathing, vagal stimulation, memory reconsolidation and HERA, lend primary support for our hypothesis that Recapitulation is one of the practices that can aid in the enhancement of perception and expansion of awareness. Here, we present the results of literature searches in these areas that provide relevant evidence supporting the first part of our hypothesis which claims; Recapitulation improves various cognitive processes associated with perception through training.

Enhancing Perception

According to the first part of our hypothesis, *Recapitulation* is another practice advocated by Castaneda, that, through regular training, can improve the essential process/functions associated with perception, including memory, attention and volition.

Memory is an essential process/function of perception that can be improved in two significant ways by the practice of Recapitulation. First, memory reconsolidation provides a powerful mechanism to figuratively *clear the clutter from our personal history*, to change the contents of our "giant memory warehouse", and consequently change all the "feelings, ideas, mental dialogues and behavior patterns" which have been stored within us as a personal inventory (1 p. 74). Essentially, Recapitulation provides a means to alter memory and change fixed values, judgments, ideas, dialogues and behaviors that limit, confine or restrict awareness, and in doing so, fundamentally change perception. Second, Recapitulation practice, like MEmory Specificity Training, can enhance memory recall and specifically autobiographical memory. This conclusion is based on MEST research (6) (8) which indicates that the systematic practice of autobiographical memory retrieval can improve autobiographical memory performance. MEST research has also shown a potential to reduce vulnerability to depression (9) (6) and improve PTSD symptoms (10).

We suggest that Recapitulation involves the same activity as MEST, since both methods require the participant to "recall as much (spatio-temporal, contextual, and sensory perceptual) details as possible." The ability to improve memory performance, specifically the recollection of particular and detailed autobiographical memories, resulting from repeated memory retrieval practice, is consistent with Castaneda's (3 p. 106) claim that the detailed recollection enacted during Recapitulation is the means to "hone one's capacity to remember".

And while there is presently no definitive explanation as to why Memory Specificity Training reduces PTSD symptoms and vulnerability to depression, the improvements in autobiographical memory recall do appear to *diminish the influence of affect-laden memories* (e.g. post-traumatic stress) on perception and behavior (10). When stated in this manner, both of Castaneda's (2 pp. 147-148) declarations regarding Recapitulation seem to be quite accurate – specifically that Recapitulation practice is both a "means to hone one's capacity to remember" and a method to reduce the perceptual influence of "heavily loaded emotions".

In addition, Belleville (11) found that test subjects, with mild cognitive impairment, were able to improve episodic memory performance through participation in a cognitive intervention program. The intervention program included computer-assisted attentional training, episodic memory training, techniques to improve visual imagery abilities and working with mental maps of their home environment. This study supports the notion that Recapitulation practice can improve memory performance, since the study found *relaxation* and *mental imagery* training to be particularly beneficial in improving memory performance. Relaxation and mental imagery are both central elements in Recapitulation practice.

Research by Buss (12), exposes the detrimental effects of stress, and specifically the stress hormone, cortisol, has on autobiographical memory performance. Consequently, relaxation techniques that reduces stress and lower cortisol levels, such as those used in Recapitulation (e.g. slow-paced breathing and vagal stimulation), improve autobiographical memory performance. As Buss (12) notes, the hippocampus is believed to play a central role in autobiographical memory, therefore it is likely involved in the detrimental effects of cortisol.

Furthermore, while there is currently no evidence to indicate the presence of Vagal Nerve Stimulation (VNS) resulting from the performance of the "cleansing" breath, the act of turning the head from side-to-side undoubtedly massages the vagal nerves running vertically along each side of the neck by alternately stretching/compressing the tissues surrounding the left and right vagal nerves. Indeed, medical science employs a procedure, known as a *vagal maneuver*, or sometimes called a *carotid sinus massage*, that entails simply massaging the vagal nerves on the side of the neck. In addition, deep diaphragmatic breathing, or slow-paced breathing, can also stimulate the vagus nerve. Vagal Maneuvers, such as carotid sinus massage, diaphragmatic breathing, or slow-paced breathing are often used to slow down, or relax the heart, because one function of the vagus nerve is to elicit a state of calm and relaxation, including reducing the heart rate.

Hassert (13) identifies evidence implicating Vagal Nerve Stimulation as a mechanism that benefits cognitive processing and particularly memory consolidation and learning. Specifically, stimulating the vagus nerve, "releases the neurotransmitter norepinephrine into the amygdala, strengthening memory storage in limbic regions of the brain that regulate arousal, memory and feeling responses to emotionally laden stimuli" (14). Consequently, turning the head during the "cleansing" breath used in Recapitulation, likely benefits memory and cognitive processing in a manner similar to VNS. The important point here is that vagal nerve stimulation activates the amygdala, influencing memory consolidation (13), and likewise the memory *re-consolidation* process that is important to Recapitulation.

The amygdala consists of two bilateral brain regions primarily involved in regulating memory consolidation, decision-making, and emotional reactions. Indeed, Nader (15) suggests the amygdala is directly involved in the reconsolidation of emotional memories after they are reactivated. Therefore, we theorize that the conjunction of these three VNS actions; *calm relaxation*, *activation of the amygdala*, and *enhanced consolidation*, play a key role in the "cleansing" action of the Recapitulation breath.

> … a body of evidence exists demonstrating that activity in vagal afferent fibers influences the functioning of central nuclei that regulate the consolidation and retention of newly learned information.

We assert that memory enhancements, resulting from Recapitulation practice, are based on: 1) Memory Specificity Training, because it has been shown to enhance autobiographical memory recall; 2) reconsolidation, because it provides a powerful mechanism to change the contents of our "giant memory warehouse" - in effect, cleansing emotionally laden memories and stagnant beliefs; and 3) relaxation techniques, such as solitude, breathing and vagal stimulation, since they can improve recall by reducing the detrimental effects of stress.

While MEST is still in its infancy, limited testing appears to support the potential for practice to improve autobiographical recall. Likewise, there is still much to be learned about memory reconsolidation. However, research thus far indicates memory reconsolidation is a potentially powerful process for altering long-term memory. And when reconsolidation is coupled with relaxation techniques like slow-paced or diaphragmic breathing and vagal nerve stimulation, the potential for revamping memory extends to *emotional memory* and *decision-making*, by involving the amygdala. Reconsolidation then becomes a process that can 'cleanse' *affect-laden memories* and *psychological traumas* of their powerful influence over perception and behavior. The influential role of value-laden memory, in perception, cannot be overstated (Edelman's *remembered present*). We will address this topic further, when we discuss re-consolidation in greater detail.

Attention is another essential process/function of perception that can be improved by the *focused attention* aspect of Recapitulation. As previously mentioned, Recapitulation shares many similarities with Focused Attention Meditation because both entail *voluntarily focusing attention on a chosen object in a sustained fashion.* As all neophyte meditation practitioners quickly realize, attention wanders and must be brought back to the item of focus, time and time again. It is the act of: becoming aware of mind wandering; returning attention to the object of focus; and sustaining it, over and over, that enables attention to become less sensitive to distractions and more easily sustained, effectively developing the skills of directing, focusing and sustaining attention. In essence, attention can be trained through practice. Research indicates that expert meditators differ from non-meditators, in both their attentional ability, and their brain structure (16).

> Several recent studies have reported expertise-related changes in attentional processing and brain structures in those proficient in [focused attention] meditation.

Similarly, Brefczynski-Lewis (17) found that expert meditators, versus novice meditators, had greater brain activity "in regions related to response inhibition and attention". The authors propose brain plasticity as the possible mechanism for the neural changes that improve attention.

Likewise, MacLean (18) reports that intensive meditation training can enhance the ability to sustain attention.

> Our results add to a growing body of evidence that meditation training can improve aspects of attention...

Additionally, Manna (19) concluded that mentally practicing *focused attention* results in "functional reorganization of brain activity patterns", in the prefrontal cortex and insula, that are associated with neuroplastic changes in the brain.

Notably, the insulae are believed to be involved in consciousness and play a role in diverse functions usually linked to emotion and the regulation of the body's homeostasis. These functions include perception, motor control, self-awareness, cognitive functioning, and interpersonal experience. (20)

Furthermore, Manna (19) found expert meditators demonstrated the ability to "control cognitive engagement in conscious processing of sensory-related, thought and emotion contents". This ability suggests "that extensive training in FA meditation might improve the abilities to sustain attention focus on a particular object and to control the flow of items being attended for conscious access." Recapitulation, like focused attention meditation, requires the practitioner to focus and sustain attention on mental recollections, despite potential distractions in thought patterns or the surrounding environment. Consequently, we expect extensive practice in Recapitulation to produce similar improvements in the abilities to direct and sustain attention.

Goleman (21 p. 168), in describing the essence of focus training, suggests an analogy between mental facilities and muscles, to illustrate that mental faculties, like muscles, can develop and get stronger with practice. It is the repeated effort of bringing attention back to the object of focus that 'exercises' the 'muscles' of attention.

Volition, in addition to memory and attention, is also an essential process/function of perception that can be improved by Recapitulation practice. Specifically, *volition*, or *will*, can be enhanced by the *focused attention* aspect of Recapitulation. James (22 pp. 561-562) tells us that "Volitional effort is effort of attention" and "Effort of attention is thus the essential phenomenon of will". In other words, volitional effort is the operational mechanism that enables one to direct, focus and sustain attention. Consequently, Focused Attention meditation not only enhances the sensitivity and selectivity of attention, but also enhances the ability of volition to direct and sustain attention.

Research summarized by Schwartz (23) shows powerful evidence for a "mental force" – (a.k.a. volitional effort, will, intention, and executive function) – that can dramatically remodel areas of the brain through neural plasticity. After years of research on Obsessive Compulsive Disorder (OCD), Schwartz (23 p. 360) found that patients who consistently practiced directing their attention away from intrusive thought patterns began to rewire their brain circuits and alter the neural circuits believed to be involved in OCD.

Schwartz (23 p. 325) elegantly summarizes his agreement with James that the effective role of will is 'sustaining the contents of attention'.

> The essential achievement of the will is to attend to one object and hold it clear and strong before the mind, letting all others – its rivals for attention and subsequent action – fade away like starlight swamped by the radiance of the sun.

Heeren (24) investigated the effects of mindfulness training on executive processes and autobiographical memory specificity. Subjects that lack the ability to recall specific autobiographical memories are said to suffer from over-general memory bias. Heeren's results confirm other studies "demonstrating that [over generalized memory] bias can be changed by psychological interventions." Notably, Heeren (24) recognizes that executive resources are required to maintain attention on the specifics of episodic memories in order to recall detail. Recapitulation also requires the practitioner to maintain focus on the specifics of recalled memories. Furthermore, Heeren (24) declares that executive resources, which he labels as *cognitive flexibility*, are the facility that enables the practitioner to disengage attention from over generalized memories, and instead, engage attention on specific episodes of memory.

In agreement with the findings of Schwartz (23), Heeren (24) makes clear that *intention,* and *cognitive flexibility* can be enhanced through mindfulness training. Indeed, Heeren, like Schwartz, found that mindfulness training can be used to replace habitual responses with intentional responses. The ability to choose intentional responses, over habitual ones, is the essence of volition.

As mentioned at the beginning of this section on *Enhancing Perception*, peer reviewed research on Recapitulation is completely lacking at this time. However, Recapitulation shares many similarities with *meditation*, *MEmory Specificity Training (MEST), slow-paced breathing* and *memory reconsolidation*. Research in each of these areas indicate that Recapitulation practice can improve the performance of memory, attention and volition, the essential process/functions of perception. Therefore, a variety of research supports the first part of our hypothesis which asserts that *Recapitulation* can improve various cognitive processes associated with perception through training.

Reducing Attachments

The enhancement of perceptual abilities, such as memory, attention and volition, is only one step toward freeing awareness and enabling it to shift into a realm of new possibilities. In order to utilize enhanced perception, the attachment of perception to the daily world must be broken, particularly our attachment to the "self". As long as perception is fixated on, and bound to the "self" and the daily world, there is no possibility of perceiving anything beyond it. In other words, perception must acquire some degree of fluidity, in order to move away from the fixations of daily life. Recapitulation is a tool that can systematically free perception from the chains of daily life.

As previously described, Recapitulation has three essential components; a place of solitude, detailed recollections and the "cleansing" breath. The first component, the place of solitude, provides a supportive environment for recollecting. The physical act of temporarily withdrawing from the daily world, into a place of solitude, provides a reprieve from the demands of the daily world. Distractions caused by work, family and even our senses can be temporarily suspended by retreating into a place of solitude. Indeed, Wais (25) found that visual stimuli interfere with, and decrease the accuracy of, memory retrieval.

This finding supports Castaneda's (4 p. 288) assertion that recollecting is "easy if one can reduce the area of stimulation around the body."

Tart (26) describes how psychological energy is freed by retreating to a quiet place and lying down with eyes closed. The reduction in loading stabilization, described by Tart, is valid for Recapitulation even though it is generally performed in a seated position instead of lying down. Indeed, we act to unload the psychological burden of our daily world every time we go to bed in the evening because we retreat to a quiet place, lie down, close our eyes, and try to let go of the daily world.

Furthermore, small spaces, like those described by Castaneda (4 p. 284) and Abelar (1 pp. 57, 240) for Recapitulation, can elicit feelings of intimacy, comfort and security – they can become a place of personal refuge. Psychologist Dorothy Einon (27) describes how the sense of security, resulting from a small space, can open us up to "let go of pent-up feelings". This attribute of small spaces is ideal for Recapitulation.

> Although we require more freedom of movement as we grow up, the comfort of being contained never disappears. While a small space without an easy escape can be claustrophobic, one with an easy exit gives us enough security to let go of pent-up feelings.

Perhaps our feelings of intimacy, comfort and security for small spaces, arise from a conditioning of the nervous system that occurs during the nine months we spend in the womb or the numerous months we spend cradled by loving arms. Notably, Grandin (28) developed a "hug machine" that can achieve general calming effects as well as reduce anxiety and tension, in both adults and children with autism. She developed her idea for a "hug machine" after observing how a *squeeze chute* immediately calmed down cattle during inoculation, after pressure was applied. Similarly, many people find that swaddling a baby, or clothing a pet in snug clothing such as a *ThunderShirt*, can reduce anxiety.

These findings support the idea that a place of solitude, particularly small, out-of-the-way spaces, can provide a sense of comfort, security and relaxation, as well as a reprieve from a multitude of distractions, thereby freeing perceptual resources to enable detailed memory recall.

However, the place of solitude used for Recapitulation practice simply provides a supportive environment for the second component of Recapitulation: the recollection of detailed episodes of personal history (episodic-autobiographical memory). As previously mentioned, memories recalled in sufficient detail become volatile and subject to change during a short period of time after recall – *the reconsolidation window*. Following its volatile state, a memory undergoes a consolidation process again, aptly termed re-consolidation. When the memory is re-consolidated, it is consolidated again, in its new form, *with changes that occurred while it was in its labile state*. In Recapitulation, the recalled memories are re-consolidated with the feelings of safety, security, calm and relaxation.

Rothbaum (29) found that a modified form of Prolonged Exposure therapy, initiated within hours after a traumatic event, reduced post-traumatic stress reaction in patients exposed to a traumatic event. The modified form of Prolonged Exposure Therapy entailed the survivors confronting their anxiety by recounting the traumatic event in a 'safe' environment, and included breath training, imaginal exposure and imaginal exposure homework. Recounting the event, relaxed breathing and imaginal exposure are all elements of Recapitulation. Rothbaum (29) suggests that the modified Prolonged Exposure intervention prevents the development of PTSD "by encouraging engagement with the trauma memory and providing an opportunity for fear habituation and processing of unhelpful cognitions, thus modifying the memory before it is consolidated." Furthermore, according to reconsolidation studies, detailed recollection can also place a *previously* consolidated memory into a labile state similar to a newly acquired memory, thus enabling traumatic memories, and even long term memories, to be reconsolidated in a modified form (30) (31) (32) (33) (34). Therefore, the reconsolidation aspect of memory recall reveals the potential of Recapitulation to produce results similar to Prolonged Exposure Therapy.

One particular study, that demonstrates the power of Recapitulation, is the research performed by Schiller (34). The study strongly supports Recapitulation practice as a powerful method to 'cleanse' heavy emotions, hopes and fears attached to memories because reconsolidation provides "a window of opportunity to rewrite emotional memories."

> We provide evidence that old fear memories can be updated with non-fearful information provided during the reconsolidation window.

Because the reconsolidation process provides a powerful mechanism for updating, or changing, long-term memory, it can be used to create fundamental changes in perception. To understand how reconsolidation can create fundamental changes in perception, we need to recognize that memory provides the reference framework for perceptual identification and association, and that emotional memories exert a particularly powerful influence on perception.

Abelar (1 p. 74) wrote that we are like "a giant memory warehouse" which holds all the "feelings, ideas, mental dialogues and behavior patterns" which have been stored within us as a personal inventory. In essence, our perception draws from our "memory warehouse" to identify, associate and interpret what our senses detect around us. In this way, we are limited in what is "possible and permissible" to perceive; limited by the contents of our memory warehouse. As Abelar (1 p. 73) succinctly puts it, "the world is a huge screen of memories". In other words, when we look at the world, what we see is a scene that is constructed using our memories. In the words of Butterworth (35 p. 50), "You see things not as *they* are, but as *you* are. Your perception is shaped according to your previous experiences...".

As previously discussed, the idea that memory, specifically personal history, is used in the construction of the world that we see around us, is also supported by contemporary neuroscience. Specifically, Edelman and Tononi (36 p. 217) describe three significant characteristics of consciousness; 1) it constructs an "informative scene", 2) present reality - "the remembered present"- is a constructed scene that is connected to individual history and 3) the history of each individual is laden with value. In other words, present reality is a scene constructed using our memory – our "value-ridden" personal history.

Therefore, because items are drawn from our "memory warehouse" to assemble an "informative scene", memory plays a vital role in constructing "present reality" (a.k.a. "the remembered present"). Consequently, changes to the contents of the "memory warehouse" result in changes in the construction of "present reality". In other words, changes in memory, particularly episodic-autobiographical memory, can create changes in perception. Nowhere is the power of memory over perception more obvious than in subjects with Alzheimer's Disease. Without the necessary memories, familiar places, tasks and faces are rendered strange and unknown. Memory is an essential component in rendering the world we perceive.

Furthermore, there is evidence to indicate that emotions and emotional memories, exert a particularly powerful and wide spread influence on perception. Dolan (37) cites a variety of studies supporting the idea that emotion, via the amygdala, modulates various aspects of cognition, and specifically exerts influence on perceptual processes such as memory, attention, decision making and belief.

Dolan (37) attributes the "emotional modulation of cognition" to an "emotional-perceptual-memory circuit" that exists in the human brain. The circuit consists of the amygdala and "extensive connections" to the visual cortex and hippocampus, allowing the "amygdala to modulate their function and facilitate perceptual and memory functions in those regions." Because the recollection of emotional memories activates the amygdala, the reconsolidation that occurs during Recapitulation provides a powerful opportunity to change emotional memories, "cleanse" emotional traumas and consequently create fundamental changes in perception and belief.

While reconsolidation presents a "window of opportunity" to change emotional memories, it is the "cleansing breath" that acts to reduce anxiety and stress, and engender the feelings of relaxation and calmness that can 'update' a recalled memory before it is consolidated again. Specifically, the "cleansing breath" is a slow, rhythmic breathing pattern synchronized with turning the head from side-to-side. The "cleansing breath" elicits a state of calmness in the body that 'updates' the recollected memory with new emotional information, and the reduction in anxiety and stress is particularly beneficial to the reconsolidation process since stress has been shown to impair the recollection and reconsolidation of autobiographical memories (38).

A slow, rhythmic, breathing pattern, such as the one used in Recapitulation, has been associated with decreased heart rate, decreased blood pressure, and increased parasympathetic activity (39) (40) (41). Together, the parasympathetic and sympathetic nervous systems comprise the Autonomic Nervous System (ANS). They operate in a complementary fashion, with the sympathetic nervous system being primarily activated during states of stress and anxiety, and the parasympathetic system being primarily activated during states of calm and relaxation. The vagus nerve is an integral part of the parasympathetic nervous system.

The Defense Centers of Excellence for Psychological Health and Traumatic Brain Injury provides a thorough review (42) of various mind-body practices intended to regulate the autonomic nervous system, including slow-paced breathing, meditation and visualization. The review, titled *Mind Body Skills for Regulating the Autonomic Nervous System*, concludes that slow-paced breathing can effectively manage feelings of anxiety and stress, as well as "increase resting heart rate variability, which has been found to be associated with greater feelings of calmness and parasympathetic activity."

> As Clark and Hirschman elucidate, "It is thought that respiratory activity exerts a significant regulatory effect on cardiac activity and that because high heart rate and high respiration is often linked to anxiety, by slowing down respiration (which slows heart rate), one can lower anxiety…"
>
> ... Mounting research indicates that slow breathing holds potential to help regulate anxiety as well as facilitate improvements in cognitive functioning, especially during times of anxiety and excessive stress.

Based on the descriptions of Recapitulation practice, provided by Abelar and Castaneda, we find ample evidence in the literature to support our hypothesis that Recapitulation can reduce attachments to the patterns and routines of ordinary daily awareness. First, Recapitulation places the practitioner in a place of solitude, isolating them from the patterns and routines of daily life - granting a temporary reprieve from the stress and anxiety of the daily world. Second, Recapitulation can 'cleanse' the practitioner's memory warehouse of heavy emotions, hopes and fears, consequently freeing awareness from routine behaviors, repetitive thought patterns and stagnant beliefs. Slow-paced breathing and vagal stimulation induce the state of low anxiety and calm-relaxation necessary to 'cleanse' and 'update' the memories recollected during Recapitulation. Furthermore, an attitude of non-attachment and non-reactive monitoring is developed as a result of repeated exposure to value-laden memories of autobiographical episodes, while simultaneously experiencing an embodied state of safety, security, calm and relaxation. Through the use of solitude, memory reconsolidation, and relaxation, Recapitulation practice can systematically release awareness from the powerful influence of *value laden personal history* that automatically and repetitively constructs our perception of present reality. In essence, Recapitulation can effectively free awareness from constraints that bind it to the fixed perception that is the ordinary daily world.

Activating New Possibilities

The third part of our hypothesis asserts that Recapitulation is a practice that can activate new possibilities for perception that that lie beyond the boundaries of routine daily awareness. The phrase, *new possibilities*, refers to opportunities for perception to organize, identify and interpret the *energy at large* in new ways. In other words, to see the world through new eyes; to become aware of things previously disregarded; to perceive the truly novel and even experience the unknown. Huxley (43 p. 9) expounds on the idea of *new possibilities*, describing them as "something more than, and above all something different from, the carefully selected utilitarian material which our narrowed, individual minds regard as a complete … picture of reality."

In reaching for *new possibilities*, shaman found the perception of the left-body (right hemisphere) to be useful. Castaneda (3 pp. 139-140) (44 p. 167) tells us that the shaman of ancient Mexico saw that human beings are "composed of two complete functioning bodies", and they used that fundamental division as an opportunity to effectively employ the left body (right hemisphere) in seeking *new possibilities*.

When we consider the Hemispheric Encoding/Retrieval Asymmetry (HERA) model (45) (46), we find that Recapitulation preferentially activates portions of the right hemisphere (left body) during retrieval of episodic memories.

> The hemispheric encoding/retrieval asymmetry (HERA) model is a process-specific description of experimental data provided by a large set of functional neuroimaging studies. According to HERA, left prefrontal cortex (PFC) is more involved than right PFC in episodic memory encoding, whereas right PFC is more involved than left PFC in episodic memory retrieval.

Additionally, when memory recall includes emotional content and self-related processing, the right prefrontal cortices are prominently activated (47 pp. 390, 392).

Indeed, a meta-analysis of autobiographical memory recall (48) concluded that the right hemisphere is preferentially involved in emotional processing.

> The additional recruitment of right hemisphere brain regions in emotional re-experiencing is consistent with other findings across numerous domains suggesting preferential right hemisphere involvement in emotional processing and in social cognitive processes.

Consequently, episodic memory recall, including its emotional and self-referential aspects, preferentially activate portions of the right hemisphere, potentially stimulating various hemispheric characteristics that support new perceptual possibilities, such as; broad and open attention, non-verbal imagistic thinking, enhanced creativity, novel associations, divergent thinking, and apprehension of anything new (49 pp. 27, 190, 42, 41, 50, 40).

Because Recapitulation preferentially activates portions of the right hemisphere, it is important to consider the characteristics of the right hemisphere that can support *new possibilities*. The general differences ascribed to the left and right hemispheres by McGilchrist (49 p. 229), include the left hemisphere's relationship with the world, which is primarily based on sequential processing, classification, analysis and language. The left hemisphere's viewpoint depends on language and rationality - both closed and self-referential systems, neglecting anything outside its purview. McGilchrist (49 p. 229) cautions against "the difficulty of escape from a self-enclosed system."

And while the left hemisphere view is narrow, circular, and self-referential, the right hemisphere offers an avenue for awareness to escape from the self-enclosed system created by the left hemisphere. In the words of McGilchrist (49 p. 163), "It is the task of the right hemisphere to carry the left beyond, to something new, something 'Other' than itself."

Likewise, Castaneda (3 p. 141) described the energy of the right body (left hemisphere) as circular, boring, and not allowing any expansion or anything new. Indeed, Castaneda (3 p. 140) makes it clear that the shaman of ancient Mexico, "considered [the left body] to be the most effective… for the ultimate goals of shamanism."

In addition to enabling new perceptual possibilities by stimulating right hemisphere characteristics, Recapitulation also opens awareness to new possibilities by reducing attachments to memories, and particularly emotionally laden episodes, that keep awareness confined to the same patterns, routines and consequently the same perceptual view. Like the French proverb says, 'Where the goat is tethered, there it must wander' (50 p. 4).

Memory plays a such vital and integral role in perception, from both a cognitive and neurological perspective, that changes in memory can result in perceptual changes. Chapter 1 provides a simple diagram of the process-abilities associated with perception, illustrating the involvement of memory in constructing the reality we perceive. Baars (51 p. 240) provides a similar diagram, "A functional framework", that illustrates similar components such as sensory processing, memory, attention and executive functions leading to actions and responses. Baars (51 p. 240) further delineates the various forms of stored memories, knowledge and skills, as well as working storage, that combine with top-down attention to render conscious content. The diagram provided by Baars illustrates the profoundly integrated role that memory plays in consciousness and perception.

Indeed, it is phrases such Abelar's "the world is a huge screen of memories" and Edelman's "remembered present" that hint at the truly fundamental role that memories play in interpreting the energy emanating from the environment. Bressler (52 pp. 121-126) appears to agree with Abelar & Edelman when he declares that knowledge about the environment is actively constructed using pre-existing neurocognitive structures (knowledge, memory, experience).

> Cognitive structures are organized systems of information that embody the knowledge used to construct an individual's reality.

Edelman (36 p. 137) exposes the dominant role of knowledge, memory and experience – "the previously experienced neural system" – in interpreting information from the environment, but asserting that energies from the environment (extrinsic signals) primarily convey information by creating changes in the *experienced* neural network.

> …extrinsic signals convey information not so much in themselves, but by virtue of how they modulate the intrinsic signals exchanged within a previously experienced neural system.

Similarly, Winograd and Flores (53 p. 42) cite the work of Maturana in describing the structure of the nervous system - the relations within a neuronal network - as the primary determinant of how the system reacts to any disturbance (e.g. light striking the retina).

> … The perturbations do not determine what happens in the nervous system, but merely trigger changes of state. It is the structure of the perturbed system that determines, or better, specifies what structural configurations of the medium can perturb it.

In Maturana's terms, it is experience and memory (personal history) that form neurocognitive structures and, in turn, it is those structures that determine responses to the environment (e.g. perturbations). Therefore, changes in memory, result in changes in neural structures and consequently changes in the organism's response. The changed structures "lead to patterns of activity different from those that would have been generated…". And while Maturana is hesitant to associate changes in *perception* with those changed "patterns of activity", it is indeed those patterns of activity that we do call *perception*. In this way, we can see that changes in memory can result in perceptual changes. Again, "You see things not as *they* are, but as *you* are. Your perception is shaped according to your previous experiences..." (35 p. 50)

Castaneda (54 p. 49) concurs that what exists "out there" is real, in the sense that the environment has an energetic basis, but what we perceive in our mind is determined by what we have learned (e.g. knowledge, memory, experience).

Because of memory's fundamental role in interpreting and giving meaning to the environment, the *loss of memories* can change the way we see the world (e.g. amnesia, Alzheimer's), just as the *acquisition of memories* (e.g. formal learning, personal experience) can also change the way we see the world. For example, in Schiller's (34) important work, human subjects were shown blue and yellow colored squares. The participants were conditioned to fear the yellow colored square by pairing it with a mild electric shock. Once the fear memory was established, presentation of a yellow colored square, but not a blue colored square, continued to evoke a fear response, even without the electric shock. The newly acquired memory, changed the participants perception of the yellow colored square. In other words, before the experiment, participants had a neutral response to both the yellow and blue squares. But after they acquired the new memory, created by pairing the yellow square and the electric shock, the participants demonstrated a fear response to a yellow square, even when no shock accompanied the yellow square. Participants could no longer experience the yellow square in the same way they had experienced it prior to the newly acquired memory. Their perception was changed by the newly acquired memory.

More importantly, Schiller's (34) study demonstrates how reconsolidation can be used "as an update mechanism … to alter emotional memories with new information" and to consequently change perception. Specifically, Schiller (34) demonstrated the ability to update old fear memories "with non-fearful information provided during the reconsolidation window" and selectively alter only the reactivated memories. In essence, the participants were able to change their perception of the yellow square, back to a neutral response, by using reconsolidation to alter the fear memory associated with the yellow square. In essence, the change in memory, again caused a change in perception. As Schiller's research demonstrates, Recapitulation provides all the mechanisms necessary to alter the items of our memory warehouse by updating memories with a calm, relaxed and detached perspective.

In another area of research, Gray (55) cites the *rewind technique*, as an effective intervention to "rewrite memory". Like Recapitulation, the *rewind technique* is a reconsolidation protocol that also employs relaxation and visualization to achieve long term changes to memory.

In neurobiological terms, perception is constrained by pre-existing neurocognitive structures (memories, knowledge, beliefs, behaviors, etc.). The combination of fixed long-term memories, routine behaviors, repetitive thought patterns and stagnant beliefs create a predominantly static and perceptually closed system. However, Recapitulation presents a method to modify memories and consequently create changes in neuronal structures, thereby opening perception to new possibilities. In other words, cleansing our memories of their heavily loaded emotions, opens our awareness to perceive the world around us in new ways.

Furthermore, another area of research called Reminiscent Therapy (a.k.a. Life Review Therapy) is also similar to Recapitulation practice in that both involve the detailed recollection of personal history, in a positive or neutral environment. Studies of Reminiscent Therapy have shown positive effects on depression and psychological well-being (56) (9) (57). These studies do not directly address Recapitulation practice, but they are particularly relevant when we consider the interdependence of emotion and attention. Indeed, Wadlinger (58) points out the influence that emotions can wield over attention, noting that positive emotions (like those resulting from Life Review Therapy) may *expand the breadth of attention and increase attentional flexibility*. Based on its similarity to Reminiscent Therapy, Recapitulation practice may also show positive effects on depression and well-being, resulting in an expansion in the breadth of attention and an increase in attentional flexibility, thereby enabling new possibilities for perception.

The third part of our hypothesis asserts that Recapitulation is a practice that can activate new possibilities for perception that that lie beyond the boundaries of ordinary daily awareness. In support of our hypothesis, we find that HERA research indicates activation of the right prefrontal cortex with "preferential right hemisphere involvement in emotional processing" during episodic, and particularly emotional memory retrieval. Characteristics of the right hemisphere, such as; decreased inhibition, broad and open attention, enhanced creativity, novel associations, and apprehension of anything new can significantly contribute to new perceptual possibilities. In addition, other areas of study indicate that reminiscent tasks can decrease depression and increase positive mood, and thereby broaden the breadth and flexibility of attention. And finally, we believe that regular Recapitulation practice can release emotional energy from an individual's *value laden personal history* (episodic memories) and free perception from the constraints of personal history. As a result, perception can organize, identify and interpret the *energy at large* in new ways; see the world through new eyes; become aware of things previously disregarded; perceive the truly novel and even experience the unknown.

In conclusion, Recapitulation practice, is one of the methods prescribed by Castaneda that synergistically combines solitude, detailed recollections and the "cleansing" breath, to accomplish the shaman's goal of enhancing perception and expanding awareness. Specifically, our literature search has uncovered evidence (e.g. MEST and FA Meditation) that Recapitulation improves various cognitive processes associated with perception because the *detailed episodic memory recall* and *focused attention* aspects of Recapitulation, can enhance perception by supporting improvements in memory, attention, executive function and brain plasticity.

Furthermore, evidence (e.g. memory reconsolidation, deep abdominal/slow-paced breathing and reminiscent therapy) shows that Recapitulation can reduce attachments to the patterns and routines of *ordinary daily awareness* through memory reconsolidation - a process that provides "a window of opportunity to rewrite emotional memories" and change behaviors as well as stagnant beliefs. Recapitulation provides all the elements necessary to support memory reconsolidation, and consequently alter perception. Additionally, Recapitulation employs elements such as interludes of solitude and slow-paced breathing that are conducive to reducing stress and anxiety and improving feelings of relaxation and well-being which not only support cleansing emotional memories during the reconsolidation window, but also aid in reducing attachments to patterns and routines associated with daily life. Decreases in stress and anxiety encourage new ways of perceiving by not only freeing thoughts and behaviors from repetitive and reflexive habits and routines, but also by freeing cognitive resources like memory, attention, and volition from the detrimental effects of stress and anxiety.

Moreover, we have presented evidence (e.g. HERA, reminiscent therapy and memory reconsolidation) that Recapitulation supports the activation of new possibilities for perception since the *episodic memory retrieval* aspect of Recapitulation promotes activation of the right hemisphere; the *reminiscent aspect* of Recapitulation promotes positive emotional states that can broaden and enlarge the breadth of attention; and the *reconsolidation aspect* of Recapitulation can free perception from the confines of emotional memories as well as rewrite limiting beliefs. Consequently, regular Recapitulation practice can open perception to new possibilities, by way of; broad and open attention, enhanced creativity, novel associations, divergent thinking, and apprehension of anything new.

In summary, we have presented evidence to support our hypothesis that Recapitulation is one of the practices advocated by Castaneda that can enhance perception and expand awareness; 1) by improving various cognitive processes associated with perception through training; 2) by reducing attachments to the patterns and routines of *ordinary daily awareness*; and 3) by activating new possibilities for perception that lie beyond the boundaries of *ordinary daily awareness*.

References

1. **Abelar, Taisha.** *The Sorcerers' Crossing: A Woman's Journey.* New York, NY, USA : Penguin Books USA Inc., 1992.

2. **Castaneda, Carlos.** *The Art of Dreaming.* New York, NY, USA : First HarperPerennial / HarperCollins Publishers, 1994.

3. —. *Magical Passes: The Practical Wisdom of the Shamans of Ancient Mexico.* New York, NY, USA : HarperCollins Publishers, Inc., 1998.

4. —. *The Eagle's Gift.* New York, NY, USA : Pocket Books / Washinton Square Press / Simon & Schuster, 1981.

5. **Underhill, E,.** *Practical Mysticism: A Little Book for Normal People and Abba: Mediatation Based on the Lord's Prayer.* New York, NY, USA : Vintage Books / Random House, 2003.

6. *Reducing cognitive vulnerability to depression: A preliminary investigation of MEmory Specificity Training (MEST) in inpatients with depressive symptomatology.* **Raes F, et al.** Amsterdam, Netherlands : Elsevier, 2009, Journal of Behavior Therapy and Experimental Psychiatry, Vol. 40, pp. 24-38.

7. *Memory Traces Unbound.* **Nader K.** Amsterdam, Netherlands : Elsevier, 2003, Trends in Neurosciences, Vol. 26(2).

8. *Enhancing Autobiographical Memory Specificity Through Cognitive Training: An Intervention for Depression Translated From Basic Science.* **Doost N., et al.** Thousand Oaks, CA, USA : Sage Publications, 2012, Clinical Psychological Science, Vol. XX(X), pp. 1-9.

9. *Life review therapy using autobiographical retrieval practice for older adults with clinical depression.* **Selva J., et al.** Oviedo, Asturias, Spain : Psychology Faculty of the University of Oviedo and the Psychological Association of the Principality of Asturias, 2012, Psicothema , Vol. 24(2), pp. 224-229.

10. *A pilot randomized controlled trial investigating the efficacy of MEmory Specificity Training in improving symptoms of posttraumatic stress disorder.* **Moradi A., et al.** Amsterdam, Netherlands : Elsevier, 2014, Behaviour Research and Therapy, Vol. 56, pp. 68-74.

11. *Improvement of Episodic Memory in Persons with Mild Cognitive Impairment and Healthy Older Adults: Evidence from a Cognitive Intervention Program.* **Belleville S., et al.** Basel, Switzerland : Karger, 2006, Dementia and Geriatric Cognitive Disorders, Vol. 22, pp. 486-499.

12. *Autobiographic memory impairment following acute cortisol administration.* **Buss C., et al.** Amsterdam, Netherlands : Elsevier, 2004, Psychoneuroendocrinology, Vol. 29, pp. 1093–1096.

13. *The Effects of Peripheral Vagal Nerve Stimulation at a Memory-Modulating Intensity on Norepinephrine Output in the Basolateral Amygdala.* **Hassert D., et al.** Washington DC, USA : American Psychological Association, Inc, 2004, Behavioral Neuroscience, Vol. 118(1), pp. 79–88.

14. *Stimulating the vagus nerve: memories are made of this.* **Adelson R.** Washinton DC, USA : American Psychological Association, 2004, Monitor on Psychology, Vol. 35(4).

15. *Fear memories require protein synthesis in the amygdala for reconsolidation after retrieval.* **Nader K., et al.** London, UK : Nature Publishing Group, Nature, Vol. 406, pp. 722-726.

16. *Attention regulation and monitoring in meditation.* **Lutz A., et al.** Amsterdam, Netherlands : Elsevier, 2008, Trends in Cognitive Sciences, Vol. 12(4), pp. 163-169.

17. *Neural correlates of attentional expertise in long-term meditation practitioners.* **Brefczynski-Lewis J., et al.** Washington DC, USA : US National Academy of Sciences, 2007, Proceedings of the National Academy of Sciences, Vol. 104(27), pp. 11483–11488.

18. *Intensive Meditation Training Improves Perceptual Discrimination and Sustained Attention.* **MacLean K., et al.** Thousand Oaks, CA, USA : Sage Publications, 2010, Psychological Science, Vol. 21(6), pp. 829-839.

19. *Neural correlates of focused attention and cognitive monitoring in meditation.* **Manna A., et al.** Amsterdam, Netherlands : Elsevier, 2010, Brain Research Bulletin, Vol. 82, pp. 46-56.

20. *Saliency, switching, attention and control: a network model of insula function.* **Menon V., Uddin L.** Berlin, Germany : Springer, 2010, Brain Struct ure and Function, Vols. 214(5-6), pp. 655-667.

21. **Goleman, D.** *Focus: The Hidden Driver of Excellence.* London, England, Great Britain : Bloomsbury Publishing, 2013.

22. **James, William.** *The Principles of Psychology Vol 2.* Mineola,NY, USA : Dover Publications Inc., 1950.

23. **Schwartz, Jeffrey M.** *The Mind and the Brain: Neuroplasticity and the Power of Mental Force.* New York,NY, USA : ReganBooks / HarperCollins Publishers Inc., 2003.

24. *The effects of mindfulness on executive processes and autobiographical memory specificity.* **Heeren A., et al.** Amsterdam, Netherlands : Elsevier, 2009, Behaviour Research and Therapy, Vol. 47, pp. 403-409.

25. *Neural Mechanisms Underlying the Impact of Visual Distraction on Retrieval of Long-Term Memory.* **Wais P., et al.** Washington DC, USA : Society for Neuroscience, 2010, The Journal of Neuroscience, Vol. 30(25), pp. :8541–8550.

26. *Accessing state-specific transpersonal knowledge: Inducing altered states.* **Tart C.** Palo Alto, CA, USA : Association for Transpersonal Psychology, 2008, The Journal of Transpersonal Psychology, Vol. 40(2), pp. 137-154.

27. **O'Dolan C.** http://www.juniormagazine.co.uk/baby-and-toddler/why-children-love-secret-hiding-places/2473.html. *http://www.juniormagazine.co.uk.* [Online] January 9, 2015. [Cited: July 25, 2017.]

28. *Behavioral and Physiological Effects of Deep Pressure on Children With Autism: A Pilot Study Evaluating the Efficacy of Grandin's Hug Machine.* **Edelson S., et al.** Bethesda, MD, USA : American Occupational Therapy Association, 1999, The American Journal of Occupational Therapy, Vol. 53(2), pp. 145-152.

29. *Early Intervention May Prevent the Development of PTSD: A Randomized Pilot Civilian Study with Modified Prolonged Exposure.* **Rothbaum B., et al.** Amsterdam, Netherlands : Elsevier, 2012, Biological Psychiatry, Vol. 72(11), pp. 957-963.

30. **Alberini C.** *Memory Reconsolidation.* Amsterdam, Netherlands : Academic Press / Elsevier, 2013.

31. *Characterization of Fear Memory Reconsolidation.* **Duvarci S. and Nader K.** Washingtin DC, USA : Society for Neuroscience, 2004, The Journal of Neuroscience, Vol. 24(42), pp. 9269 –9275.

32. *Memory Traces Unbound.* **Nader K.** Cambridge, MA, USA : Cell Press / Elsevier, 2003, Trends in Neurosciences, Vol. 26(2), pp. 65-72.

33. *Reconsolidation of episodic memories: A subtle reminder triggers integration of new information.* **Hupbach A., et al.** Cold Spring Harbor, NY, USA : Cold Spring Harbor Laboratory Press, 2007, Learning & Memory , Vol. 14, pp. 47-53.

34. *Preventing the return of fear in humans using reconsolidation update mechanisms.* **Schiller D., et al.** London, UK : Nature Publishing Group, 2010, Nature, Vol. 463, pp. 49-54.

35. **Butterworth E.** *Spiritual Economics.* Unity Village, MO, USA : Unity Books, 2001.

36. **Edelman, Gerald M. and Tononi, Giulio.** *A Universe of Consciousness : How Matter Becomes Immagination.* New York, NY, USA : Basic Books / Perseus Books Group, 2000.

37. *Emotion, Cognition, and Behavior.* **Dolan E.** Washington DC, USA : American Association for the Advancement of Science, 2002, Science, Vol. 298(5596), pp. 1191-1194.

38. *Stress impairs the reconsolidation of autobiographical memories.* **Schwabe L. and Wolf O.** Amsterdam, Netherlands : Elsevier, 2010, Neurobiology of Learning and Memory, Vol. 94, pp. 153-157.

39. *The Effect of Deep and Slow Breathing on Pain Perception, Autonomic Activity, and Mood Processing—An Experimental Study.* **Busch V., et al.** Hoboken, NJ, USA : Wiley-Blackwell, 2012, Pain Medicine, Vol. 13, pp. 215-228.

40. *Physiology of long pranayamic breathing: Neural respiratory elements may provide a mechanism that explains how slow deep breathing shifts the autonomic nervous system.* **Jerath R., et al.** Amsterdam, Netherlands : Elsevier, 2006, Medical Hypotheses., Vol. 67(3), pp. 566-571.

41. *Effect of short-term practice of breathing exercises on autonomic functions in normal human volunteers.* **Pal G., et al.** Mumbai, India : Medknow Publications, 2004, Indian Journal of Medical Research, Vol. 120, pp. 115-121.

42. **Moore M., et al.** *Mind-Body Skills for Regulating the Autonomic Nervous System.* Defense Centers of Excellence for Psychological Health and Traumatic Brain Injury. Silver Springs, MD, USA : DCoE, 2011.

43. **Huxley A.** *The Doors of Percpetion.* New York, NY, USA : Harper & Row, 1954.

44. **Castaneda, Carlos.** *The Active Side of Infinity.* New York, NY, USA : HarperCollins Publishers, 1998.

45. *Hemispheric encoding/retrieval asymmetry in episodic memory: Positron emission tomography findings.* **Tulkving E., et al.** Washingtin DC, USA : US National Academy of Sciences, 1994, Proceedings of the National Academy of Sciences, Vol. 91, pp. 2016-2020.

46. *Hemispheric asymmetries of memory: the HERA model revisited.* **Habib R., et al.** Amsterdam, Netherlands : Elsevier, 2003, Trends in Cognitive Sciences, Vol. 7(6), pp. 241-245.

47. **Zimmer H., et al.** *Handbook of Binding and Memory: Perspectives from Cognitive Neuroscience.* New York, NY, USA : Oxford University Press, 2006.

48. *The functional neuroanatomy of autobiographical memory: A meta-analysis.* **Svoboda E., et al.** Amsterdam, Netherlands : Elsevier, 2006, Neuropsychologia, Vol. 44(12), pp. 2189–2208.

49. **McGilchrist, Iain.** *The Master and his Emissary; The Divided Brain and the Making of the Western World.* NewHaven, CT, USA : Yale University Press, 2010.

50. **Hennel, Thomas.** *The Witnesses.* New Hyde Park, NY, USA : University Books, 1967.

51. **Baars, Bernard J. and Gage, Nicole M.** *Cognition, Brain, and Consciousness* . Burlington, MA, USA : Academic Press / Elsevier Ltd., 2007.

52. **Riegler A., et al.** *Understanding Representation in the Cognitive Sciences: Does Representation Need Reality?* New York, NY, USA : Kluwer Academic / Plenum Publishers, 1999.

53. **Winograd T.** *Understanding Computers and Cognition: New Foundation for Design.* Norwood, NJ, USA : Ablex Publishing, 1990.

54. **Castaneda, Carlos.** *The Fire from Within.* New York, NY, USA : Simon and Schuster, 1984.

55. *PTSD: Extinction, Reconsolidation, and the Visual-Kinesthetic Dissociation Protocol.* **Gray R., and Liotta R.,.** Thousand Oaks, CA, USA : Sage Publishing, 2012, Traumatology, Vol. 18(2), pp. 3-16.

56. *The effects of reminiscence therapy on psychological well-being, depression, and loneliness among the institutionalized aged.* **Chian K., et al.** Hoboken, NJ, USA : John Wiley & Sons, 2010, International Journal of Geriatric Psychiatry, Vol. 25, pp. 380-388.

57. **Bohlmeijer E.** *Reminiscence and depression in later life (Disertation).* Amsterdam, Netherlands : Faculty of Psychology and education, Vrije Universiteit, 2007.

58. *Fixing our focus: Training attention to regulate emotion.* **Wadlinger H. and Isaacowitz D.** London, UK : Sage Publishing, 2011, Personality and Social Psychology Review, Vol. 15(1), pp. 75–102.

CHAPTER 5

Dreaming

****

Castaneda (1 p. 115) wrote extensively about *dreaming*, revealing that shaman sought to make use of ordinary dreams as an "entrance for human awareness into other realms of perceiving." According to our hypothesis, *Shamanic Dreaming*, like *Magical Passes* and *Recapitulation*, is another practice described by Castaneda that provides a means for practitioners to enhance perception and expand awareness beyond the confines of ordinary daily awareness.

We have elected to use the phrase *Shamanic Dreaming* to differentiate it from ordinary night time dreaming, since, as Castaneda (1 p. 116) tells us, his teacher also used different Spanish words to distinguish between the two.

In his book, *Magical Passes*, Castaneda (1 p. 117) asserts that there are two types of dreams; *ordinary dreams* and *energy-generating dreams*. However, in his book *The Art of Dreaming*, Castaneda (2 p. 231) describes another type of dream; a type of dream that is not an *ordinary dream*, and yet it is also not an *energy-generating dream*, but a dream that is constructed by a dreamer projecting their intent.

Therefore, we will characterize three basic types of dreams (see Table 1). The first type is an *ordinary dream*, which Castaneda (1 p. 117) (2 p. 164) described as, "…the product of our mentality, our psyche; perhaps something that has to do with our neurological makeup", "…a phantom world of projections, where nothing generates energy, like most of our dreams, where nothing has an energetic effect." Hobson (3 p. 4) describes five characteristics of ordinary dreams (Table 1).

The second type of dream is called a *lucid dream*, because the dreamer has clear perception and a rational awareness, similar to that of waking consciousness. The essential characteristic of a *lucid dream* is that the dreamer is aware that they are dreaming, within the dream itself. Lucid dreamers are typically able to intentionally guide or exert some degree of control over aspects of the dream. We classify lucid dreams as neither *ordinary dreams*, nor *energy-generating dreams*, but similar to the other type of dream described by Castaneda (2 p. 231) in which the dreamer projects "… their thoughts in dreaming in order to accomplish the truthful reproduction of any object or structure or landmark or scenery of their choice." LaBerge (4 p. 109) delineates five basic characteristics of *lucid dreams* (Table 1).

The third type of dream is called an *energy-generating dream* (Table 1), because according to Castaneda (1 p. 116) the dreamer is able to perceive energy directly – energy from elements with an energetic basis – instead of perceiving merely phantom projections, like ordinary dreams. In other words, *energy-generating dreams* are perceptually based on energy, similar to the way ordinary waking perception is based on energy emanating, or reflecting, from objects.

Table 1 Characteristics of Various Dream Types

Type of Dream	Lucid	Energy Generating	Characteristics
Ordinary Dream	No	No	Intense Emotion Illogical and disorganized content Bizarre sensory impressions (e.g. falling) Uncritical acceptance of strange content Difficult to remember
Lucid Dream	Yes	No	Conscious of the dream state Freely remember waking life Think clearly Reflective awareness Act deliberately
Energy-Generating Dream	Yes	Yes	Same characteristics as lucid dreams Perception of energy-generating elements Interaction with energy-generating elements

However, Castaneda (2 p. 29) also tells us that energetic elements can get mixed with ordinary dreams. But, without the ability to distinguish *energy-generating* elements from the *products of our mentality*, everything appears as dream imagery. Therefore, Castaneda (1 pp. 120, 117) asserts that shaman deliberately seek to develop a faculty called *dreaming attention* in order to identify and isolate the energy-generating elements in dreams.

Furthermore, according to Castaneda (2 p. 70), *Shamanic Dreaming* is more than just nighttime dreaming; it is synonymous with shifting one's level of attention, or shifting one's world view, or shifting one's *assemblage point* – a point in our energetic configuration that is "key in the act of turning energy into sensory data and then interpreting it". Consequently, once the *dreaming attention* emerges and becomes functional, it can also be invoked while one is awake, enabling one to perceive the daily world using *dreaming attention* rather than the *ordinary attention* of daily awareness.

Thus, *Shamanic Dreaming* is the use of ordinary dreams to enhance perception and expand awareness into an arena of new possibilities. In particular, *Shamanic Dreaming* practices propose to develop and enhance the same perceptual process-abilities in dreaming, that are used in daily awareness, specifically memory, attention and volition. Furthermore, *Shamanic Dreaming* practices can redeploy energy resources away from the patterns and routines of daily life and toward the goal of establishing, and exercising the ability to volitionally direct attention in dreams - *dreaming attention*. Moreover, the cultivation of *dreaming attention* potentially opens awareness to new perceptual realms, and places the practitioner in a position to perceive "something more than, and above all something different from" ordinary reality.

Therefore, *Shamanic Dreaming* practices, like *Magical Passes* and *Recapitulation* practices promote an enhancement of perception, and an expansion of awareness, in the manner we have outlined as our hypothesis; 1) by improving various cognitive processes associated with perception through training; 2) by reducing attachments to the patterns and routines of *ordinary daily awareness*; and 3) by activating new possibilities for perception that lie beyond the boundaries of *ordinary daily awareness*.

Unfortunately, peer reviewed research on *Shamanic Dreaming* is completely lacking at this time. But we believe the practice shares many similarities with other research subjects such as, meditation, dream recall and lucid dreaming. Each of these areas, as well as other areas of research, has peer reviewed literature that is relevant to an assessment of *Shamanic Dreaming* practices.

Enhancing Perception

According to the first part of our hypothesis, *Shamanic Dreaming* is another practice advocated by Castaneda, that, through regular training, can enhance essential process-abilities associated with perception, including memory, attention and volition.

Memory is not only a fundamental process-ability of ordinary daily perception, but it also plays a particularly critical role in lucid dreaming and *Shamanic Dreaming*. Specifically, memory forms the essential bridge between *dreaming consciousness* and *waking consciousness*. In order to cultivate *dreaming attention*, one must first develop the ability to remember one's dreams in waking life. It is also necessary to develop the ability to remember one's waking life, or at least portions of it, while dreaming. In this way, memory forms a connecting link between *waking consciousness* and *dreaming consciousness*. Marzano (5) provides some evidence that the neural underpinnings for memory may be the same for both waking and dreaming consciousness.

If we accept the conclusion of this research, that the neural mechanisms for encoding and recalling episodic memories are the same for waking and dreaming states, then memory training in waking states, and the resulting improvements, also benefit encoding and recall in dreaming states. Indeed, several lucid dreaming techniques rely on this phenomenon and therefore lucid dreamers suggest various practices to be performed in waking consciousness, including dream recall and prospective memory practice.

Lucid dreaming shares many characteristics with *Shamanic Dreaming*. Specifically, lucid dreaming and *Shamanic Dreaming*, both require the dreamer to be conscious of the dream state, freely remember waking life, think clearly, possess some degree of reflective awareness and even act volitionally.

Research (6) (7) (8) (9) (10) confirms that lucid dreaming is a learnable skill. Therefore, *Shamanic Dreaming* is also learnable, since it employs many of the same skills necessary for lucid dreaming. In the case of lucid dreaming, practitioners typically begin enhancing memory by improving dream recall and prospective memory. Likewise, Castaneda also began with a task that fostered the development of dream recall and prospective memory.

At the beginning of his training in *Shamanic Dreaming*, Castaneda (2 p. 21) was given the task of finding and looking at his hands in his dreams. This task fostered the development of his memory by requiring him: 1) to remember his dreams in waking life – to confirm that he had found his hands in dreaming and, 2) to remember his waking life intention – to look at his hands, while he was dreaming.

The exercise, of looking at one's hands while in a dream state, engages two aspects of memory. First, the practitioner must develop *dream recall* – the ability to remember one's dreams in waking life (e.g. recall having looked at one's hands while in a dream). Second, the practitioner must develop *prospective memory* – the ability to remember to perform a planned action at some future point in time (e.g. look at their hands while they are dreaming).

Research regarding dream recall has uncovered several factors that positively influence dream recall, such as; attitude toward dreams, recall practice and body position. Specifically, Bachner (11) found that parents asking about children's dreams, as well as sharing their own dreams, positively influenced dream recall frequency and attitude towards dreams, when those children reached adulthood. Additional research (12) (13) supports the conclusion that expectancy and attitude towards dreams can have a positive effect on dream recall. Furthermore, a meta-analysis by Beaulieu-Pre'vost (14) of 24 different studies on dream recall frequency confirmed that a positive attitude toward dreams increases dream recall frequency.

These studies may partially explain the success of dream journals in improving dream recall, since a commitment to the regular use of a dream journal generally indicates interest and a positive attitude toward dreams. Notably, dream journals are a highly-recommended strategy by LaBerge (15 pp. 16, 37, 38) to improve dream recall for lucid dreamers. In addition, the consistent use of a dream journal implies frequent recall practice. Memory Specificity Training (MeST) (16) (17) has shown that the systematic practice of autobiographical memory retrieval that is required to keep a dream journal, can improve autobiographical memory performance. Furthermore, dream journaling helps to develop familiarity with dream content in waking consciousness, thereby creating neural networks and associations that are common to both dreaming and waking consciousness, making dream content more familiar and more easily remembered.

While Castaneda (2 p. 27) does not encourage the use of a dream journal, he admits that he kept "a meticulous, superpersonal diary called 'My Dreams'." Based on available evidence, it is very likely that Castaneda's dream journal aided his dream recall through not only the consistent practice of recalling dreams, but also by creating a positive attitude toward dreams through a welcoming mindset, excitement, interest and desire, as well as creating familiarity with his dream content.

Furthermore, Castaneda (2 p. 26) indicates that he regularly exercised his prospective memory, by doggedly practicing his intention to see his hands in his dreams. Various studies (18) (19) (20) provide evidence that prospective memory can be improved through effort and practice. Indeed, LaBerge (15 p. 76) recommends developing *prospective memory*, through daily practice, as a prerequisite for lucid dreaming. Specifically, a method for inducing lucid dreams, called Mnemonic Induction of Lucid Dreams (MILD), relies on both creating familiarity with dream content, through the use of dream journals, and using familiar dream content as a prospective memory mnemonic, to trigger the awareness that one is dreaming, and thereby become lucid. In other words, when the dreamer recognizes they are experiencing a familiar dream they can use the familiarity aspect of the dream to realize they are dreaming.

Both lucid dreaming and *Shamanic Dreaming* require enhancements in memory, which can be accomplished through effort and practice, in waking and dreaming states. Various waking practices can aid dreaming lucidity. Specifically, journaling dreams can help to improve dream recall and attitude towards dreams, while also creating waking-consciousness familiarity with dream content. In conjunction with dream journals, a daily practice for improving *prospective memory*, in waking states, can also develop opportunities to use familiar dream content as a mnemonic trigger for *prospective memory*, helping the practitioner to the realize when they are dreaming. In addition, remembering to perform a specific task in dreaming, such as looking at one's hands, also exercises prospective memory in the dream state of consciousness.

However, another intriguing aspect of memory is the association between memory retrieval and body position. Indeed, because of the interaction between body position and memory, LaBerge (15 p. 37) recommends not moving, immediately upon waking, in order to facilitate dream recall.

In support of this recommendation, Dijkstra (21) and Casasanto (22) found that body position and motor actions affect memory retrieval. And in a review of research areas related to memory encoding-retrieval, Kent (23) concludes that "retrieval is aided by behavioural re-enactment of processes involved in encoding, including re-enactment of encoding eye movements."

Additional support comes from a meta-analysis, examining memory's dependence on environmental contexts. Specifically, Smith (24) suggests that *memory* and *perception of the immediate environment*, share cognitive resources. In other words, focusing on dream content upon waking, without engaging in the immediate environment (e.g. moving or thinking about daily concerns), reduces the interference effects of the immediate environment.

Moreover, Kent (23) states that "Particularly compelling evidence for the benefits of re-enactment has been obtained in eye-movement studies, which suggest that eye movements have a functional role in retrieval."

Interestingly, Castaneda and his cohorts were aware of the functional connection between eye movement and memory. Castaneda (25 p. 308) (26 p. 258) cites various examples of using eye movement; to facilitate memory recall (e.g. looking at a specific point in space using just the eyes) as well as, to disengage from environmental cues (e.g. rolling the eyes).

Similarly, Abelar (27 p. 5) describes a technique where she regularly used her eyes to disengage from the immediate environment in order to open her perception to previously unknown options.

Clearly, memory is essential to dreaming, and particularly important to lucid and *Shamanic Dreaming*. Fortunately, there are various practices that can be used to develop and enhance memory in the waking-state of consciousness, such as regular practice in; dream recall, dream journaling, autobiographical memory retrieval and prospective memory. In addition, dreamers can practice recalling their waking-state memories, or waking-state intentions, while dreaming. These dreaming techniques, exercise, develop and enhance memory in two different states of consciousness.

In addition to memory, attention is another essential process-ability of perception that can be improved through training. Numerous studies (28) (29) (30) (31) have shown that focused attention practices produce improvements in certain aspects of attention. In a study examining the effects of Mindfulness Based Stress Reduction (MBSR) training, Jha (32) concluded that "...participation in the MBSR course improved the ability to endogenously orient attention...".

Similarly, a study conducted by Jensen (33) supports the conclusion that meditation practices produce attentional improvements. Jensen (33) specifically found that "...MBSR led to improvements in the perceptual threshold and a measure of sustained, selective attention."

Meditation research is particularly relevant because according to Castaneda (34 p. 294) (25 p. 261), shaman used a practice called *gazing* to develop attention in daily awareness, which also aided the development of *dreaming attention. Gazing* is performed by placing one's attention on an object and holding it on that object for long periods of time. If attention strays, then it is repeatedly brought back to the object of focus. *Gazing* was specifically used to develop the attention necessary for *Shamanic Dreaming.*

Gazing, like focused attention meditation and Mindfulness Training, engages the practitioner in the effort of attention; directing attention toward something (e.g. a dried leaf), selectively attending to that something, and sustaining attention on that something. In this way, the practitioner exercises directing, focusing and sustaining attention. Therefore, because the attentional exercises employed in focused attention meditation and *gazing* are so fundamentally similar, we expect that *gazing*, like focused attention mediation, also improves aspects of attention through diligent practice. However, gazing may be a type of attentional training particularly beneficial to *Shamanic Dreaming*, since *gazing* enlists the eyes to direct and hold attention on an item. Specifically, *Shamanic Dreaming* calls for the dreamer to; direct, focus and sustain attention by using their eyes; through such recommendations as looking at their hands, or maintaining their awareness "on the items of their dreams". Whereas, mindfulness-based training that focuses attention on the breath has no "object' to look at with the eyes. *Gazing*, as the name implies, may therefore aid in developing and enhancing a specific and useful association between the eyes and directed attention. Interestingly, the eyes are one of the few body parts that can be intentionally directed while dreaming. Furthermore, since *gazing* calls for visually fixating on an object, or objects, for hours, the objects are very likely to appear in one's dreams. This effect has been referred to as the Tetris Effect. The appearance of the *gazing* object(s) in one's dreams can act as a "dream sign" – a dream image that alerts the dreamer to the fact that they are dreaming.

In addition to *gazing* practices, which exercise attention during states of waking consciousness, shaman also exercise attention during states of dreaming. Specifically, practitioners doggedly try to place their attention on an object in their dreams (e.g. their hands), then focus and sustain their attention on that object. Once that is accomplished, practitioners can continue to exercise their attention by shifting it to other items in the dream. The ability to direct, focus and sustain attention, on the items of a dream, is called *dreaming attention*.

Gazing practices are therefore a technique used by shaman, to train attention in the waking-state of consciousness, while *dreaming attention* practices are a shamanic technique to train attention in the dreaming-state of consciousness. In this way, these two complementary techniques exercise, develop and enhance attention in two different states of consciousness. Indeed, *gazing* practices that develop and enhance attentional networks in the waking-state, may facilitate the development of attentional networks during the dreaming-state. Castaneda (34 p. 294) appears to support this conclusion when he declares, "dreamers have to be gazers" first.

Volition is the third essential process-ability of perception that can be improved through training. *Dreaming attention*, like ordinary attention, is guided by volition (a.k.a. will, intention). Remember that James (35 pp. 561-562) exposed the relationship between attention and volition when he concluded that:

> Volitional effort is effort of attention.
>
> The essential achievement of will … is to attend to a difficult object and hold it fast before the mind."
>
> Effort of attention is thus the essential phenomenon of will.

In his original and influential work on the mind and the brain, Schwartz (36 p. 325) expressed his agreement with James that the effective role of will is 'sustaining the contents of attention'. The research presented by Schwartz makes a strong case for volition to be regarded as a fundamental force; a mental force that can significantly alter the biological structure of the brain. Evidently, the repetitive application of mental effort to direct, focus and sustain attention, enables the practitioner to exercise and ultimately strengthen their volition.

As previously discussed, true volition emerges beyond the boundaries of habit and interest, and stands firm, in the form of intent, or will, even when it contradicts our inventory of values. Volition is more than just the habitual engagement of value, interest and importance. As William James (35 p. 559) points out, pain, pleasure, instinct, emotion and habit, all "drive other thoughts from consciousness at the same time that they instigate their own characteristic 'volitional' effects." In other words, what sometimes appears to be an act of volition is not really an act of volition at all, since the act is driven not by "free will", but by habit, simply because habit makes it the "steadfast occupancy of consciousness" and the "steadfast occupancy of consciousness" is the essential phenomenon of volition.

Ghoshal (37) similarly differentiates between motivation and volition, asserting that motivation is often "triggered by external stimuli or expectation of reward", whereas volition "implies deep personal attachment to an intention".

> Willpower lets [people] execute disciplined action even when they lack desire, expect not to enjoy the work, or feel tempted by alternative opportunities.

Castaneda (2 pp. 35-36) declares that it is persistence that ultimately gives rise to the development of *dreaming attention.* Of course, persistence, in this case, implies the action of volitional control, in a sustained or repetitive manner. Descriptive terms, such as; "persevering", "being tenacious", "continuing on", and "leaving no stone unturned", particularly in the face of unrewarded behavior, are all forms of volitional exercise.

Indeed, Castaneda (38 p. 233) describes how his teacher used a variety of nonsensical tasks to instill the idea of *acting without expectation or reward.* In these examples, we can see that Castaneda had to employ his volition rather than rely on motivation (as described by Ghoshal above). Castaneda was acting to complete these tasks, to produce results, rather than being driven by reward or expectation, since he accepted these tasks as jokes, non-sense, or absurd activities. Castaneda was not driven by a motivation for reward, and instead had to rely on his volition.

While *persistence* and *acting without reward* are relevant to developing volition, *Shamanic Dreaming* activities appear to be the central practices employed to exercise, develop and enhance volition. Holzinger (39) and LaBerge (40) recognize *volition* and *reflective awareness* as essential elements of lucid dreaming and designate them as identifying characteristics of lucid dreaming. *Shamanic Dreaming*, like lucid dreaming, is also characterized by *volitional control* and *reflective awareness*.

In an investigation examining *volition* across different states of consciousness, Dresler (41) found that lucid dreams enable the dreamer to volitionally act according to their intentions, as opposed to being a "passive subject in the chaotic flow of the dream narrative." Specifically, lucid dreaming showed a greater prevalence of *intention enactment* over both wakefulness and non-lucid dreaming.

And, using brain imaging to investigate lucid dreaming, Hobson (42), Voss (43) and Dresler (44) found neurocognitive evidence to support a conclusion that lucid dreaming does indeed involve activation of brain regions associated with *volition* and *reflective awareness*.

LaBerge (45) convincingly demonstrated the ability of lucid dreamers to exhibit volitional control and reflective awareness, through the use of volitional communication during REM sleep. In the experiment, LaBerge had lucid dreamers perform specific actions (e.g. distinguishing patterns of eye movement), once they entered into lucid dreaming, concluding "that it is possible for lucid dreamers to signal intentionally to the environment while continuing to dream."

In ordinary dreams, volitional control and reflective awareness are diminished or absent, but in lucid dreams those psychological facilities are reactivated (46). Therefore, once dream lucidity is achieved, the dreamer is in a position to exercise volition since lucidity "switches on" the frontal areas of the brain that activate volition in the dream-state. In fact, practicing to become lucid is itself an exercise in volition, because persistent effort of attention is required to develop lucidity. Since, *Shamanic Dreaming* also involves lucidity and reflective awareness, it too is a practice for improving volition and reflective awareness. And because lucid dreaming is a skill that can be acquired through practice (8) (9), *Shamanic Dreaming* is also a skill that can be acquired through practice.

Furthermore, once a state of lucidity can be regularly achieved, there are additional opportunities to practice and continue the development of volition while in the dream-state. As we shall discuss later, Castaneda (2 p. 22) describes some of the specific practices and activities, called *the seven gates of dreaming*, that progressively develop and enhance dreaming volition.

In this section on enhancing perception, we indicated a lack of peer reviewed research on *Shamanic Dreaming*. However, *Shamanic Dreaming* shares many similarities with other research subjects such as, meditation, dream recall and lucid dreaming. Research in each of these areas indicate that *Shamanic Dreaming*, and its associated practices (e.g. journaling, prospective memory training, dream recall, gazing, acting without reward, reflective awareness, lucid dreaming and volitional activity), can enhance perception by improving the performance of memory, attention and volition - the essential process-abilities of perception.

Reducing Attachments

Of course, enhancement of the perceptual processes of memory, attention and volition, is only one step toward enhancing perception and enabling awareness to shift into a realm of new possibilities. In order to utilize enhanced perception, the attachment of perception to the "self" and to the daily world must be broken. As long as perception is fixated on the "self", and bound to the daily world, there is no possibility of perceiving anything beyond it. Therefore, the second part of our hypothesis claims that *Shamanic Dreaming*, and its associated practices, can reduce attachments to the patterns and routines of ordinary daily awareness, essentially freeing awareness to experience other aspects of the energy at large.

As we shall see, the development of volition and reflective awareness resulting from the practice of *Shamanic Dreaming* can not only provide the momentary pause necessary to observe the "self", but also help to overcome the influence of instinct and the reliance on habit.

Reflective awareness is what enables dreamers to "reflect" on their current situation, to detach themselves from the flow of the dream, and to recognize that they are dreaming. LaBerge (47 p. 221) declares that reflective consciousness allows one to "reflect on possible alternatives", "respond creatively", and exercise "freedom from the compulsion of habit".

Like LaBerge, Castaneda (1 p. 16) (48 p. 74) (25 p. 307) also expressed high regard for *reflective behavior* characteristics such as adaptability, improvisation, resourcefulness, and fluidity. Castaneda not only attributed these characteristics to his teacher by noting his ability to be adaptable, flexible, resourceful, fluid and free from habit, but also regarded these characteristics as essential for shaman.

LaBerge (47 p. 220) pragmatically delineates and characterizes *reflective* behavior by placing it on an evolutionary scale and comparing it with other forms of cognition and behavior. The four varieties of cognition and behavior described by LaBerge; reflexive, instinctive, habitual and intentional, provide a clear backdrop for understanding how our energy and awareness can become fixated on the daily world - by getting trapped in the three behaviors lower on the evolutionary ladder – reflexive, instinctive, and habitual – while volition and reflective consciousness, often remain dormant, under-utilized, overwhelmed, or overridden by instinctual motivations.

The danger of consistently relying on reflex, instinct and habit, is that cognition and behavior can become dominated by instinctual motivations such as pleasure, satisfaction, fear, and pain. Indeed, the same reward mechanisms that exert a strong motivation for food and sex are also responsible for drug and alcohol addiction. [ASAM Definition of Addiction]

> Current neuroscience recognizes that the neurocircuitry of reward also involves a rich bi-directional circuitry connecting the nucleus accumbens and the basal forebrain. It is the reward circuitry where reward is registered, and where the most fundamental rewards such as food,

> hydration, sex, and nurturing exert a strong and life-sustaining influence. Alcohol, nicotine, other drugs and pathological gambling behaviors exert their initial effects by acting on the same reward circuitry that appears in the brain to make food and sex, for example, profoundly reinforcing.

For example, instinct has wired humans to prefer foods that supply resources necessary for survival; carbohydrates and sugars – as sources of quick energy, fats – as a source of high-density energy, and salts – as a source of electrolytes. Consequently, the body provides a reward of pleasure when these foods are consumed. But without self-regulation, an overabundance of these foods can lead to serious health consequences, such as; diabetes, obesity, heart disease and high blood pressure. The prevalence of these health conditions, wherever these foods are readily available, demonstrate the power and danger of unchecked instinctual motivation.

As another example, to demonstrate the power of instinct and the resultant habitual behavior, consider that instinct has wired human beings for "self-preservation", endowing them with natural mechanisms (physical and psychical) to protect and preserve their life. Castaneda (38 p. 122) portrays the self-preservation aspect of the tonal – the "protector of our life" - as a guardian, that eventually becomes a guard. Here we infer a direct correlation between the instinct of "self-preservation" and self-importance. As Castaneda describes it, the tonal is "the most important part of our lives" and because of its self-preservation aspect, all of its doings are very important, thereby justifying its elevation to a position of supreme importance- it protects our life. Consequently, self-importance is a quality that develops from the instinct of self-preservation. Self-preservation works to protect our life, but self-importance expands its domain to our social status, reputation and possessions. Self-importance often becomes a dominant factor in our lives. Many of our daily habits and routines are driven by self-importance. We habitually and routinely devote significant time and energy to elevating and/or protecting our self-image and defending it whenever it is threatened. Castaneda (26 pp. 26, 29) singled-out self-importance as the shaman's greatest enemy because it consumes too much energy. In essence, the instinct of self-preservation evolves into a variety of ego-protecting habitual behaviors that we readily, and repeatedly, rely on as we interact with our daily world.

Another example of the daily attachments associated with instinctual and habitual behavior can be found in the human instinct to procreate. To promote sexual activity, the body provides a reward of pleasure. Unfortunately, the pleasure derived from sex can motivate people to become preoccupied with sex or to seek excess. Again, the proliferation of sex, via seductive clothing, sexual accessories, physical enhancements, sexual pharmacology, and pornography, indicates the power and danger of unchecked instinctual motivations and their power to chain energy and behavior to habit and routine.

These examples of ordinary instinctual motivation; food, self-preservation and sex, frequently elicit behaviors that are motivated by pleasure or fear. Of course, repetitious behaviors readily become habit. Consequently, it is easy to slip into a life filled with habits and routines that are driven by instinct, perennially at the mercy of our environment, unable to stop and reflect on our situation or rally the energy necessary to make a change. In our daily lives, we can become trapped in patterns of habitual behavior, eating for pleasure and not nutrition, reacting to personal affronts, adorning ourselves, defending our actions, recounting stories that glorify us and seeking the pleasure of sexual stimulation and physical satisfaction. Put simply, we engage in self-indulgent behavior, in a habitual manner. Underhill (49 pp. 50, 51) describes our condition in this way.

> … if you really knew yourself--saw your own dim character, perpetually at the mercy of its environment; your true motives, stripped for inspection and measured against eternal values; your unacknowledged self-indulgences; your irrational loves and hates--you would be compelled to remodel your whole existence, and become for the first time a practical man.

***

> … the sum total of your energy, has been turned the wrong way, harnessed to the wrong machine. … Habit has you in its chains. You are not free.

Fortunately, *Shamanic Dreaming*, like lucid dreaming, focuses on the essential characteristics of volitional control and reflective awareness (39) (40). Using brain imaging to investigate lucid dreaming, Hobson (42) (46), Voss (43) and Dresler (44) found neurocognitive evidence to support a conclusion that lucid dreaming does indeed involve activation of brain regions associated with *volition* and *reflective awareness* while ordinary dreams lack these elements. In other words, achieving lucidity in dreaming indicates activation of volitional areas of the brain. Furthermore, the *gates of dreaming* described by Castaneda (2) provide a series of exercises that progressively develop and expand the range and dimension of volitional control.

Therefore, because *Shamanic Dreaming* practices aid the development and enhancement of reflective awareness and volition, they provide an essential element, not only for escaping the chains of instinctual motivation and habitual behavior that make up daily life, but also for enabling dreamers to detach themselves from the flow of events in a dream, and thereby create the conditions necessary for *dreaming attention*. As we have seen, both lucid dreaming and *Shamanic Dreaming* support the development of reflective consciousness and volitional action, enabling practitioners to free energy caught in the flow of dream activity or the routines of daily life, and to emerge from the hypnotic slumber of continual reliance on instinct and habit. In other words, reflective consciousness and volition can overcome instinctual motivations and habitual behaviors, thereby enabling the practitioner to reduce attachments to the patterns and routines of ordinary daily awareness.

Shaman also claim that sexual abstinence is a particularly important technique that not only reduces attachment to the daily world, but also aids *Shamanic Dreaming*. In general, the books written by Castaneda and Abelar recommend sexual abstinence as a way of life, particularly for shaman neophytes. Obviously, dating, courting and other pursuits of sexual gratification, occupy time, attention energy and awareness that could otherwise be directed toward alternative pursuits, such as shamanic practices. Romantic relationships and sexual encounters are also likely to produce emotional memories and attachments that can affect our perception of the world (consider Edelman's "remembered present"). Moreover, sexual activities can lead to life altering consequences, such as matrimony, emotional investments, offspring, unhealthy relationships, abuse, sexually transmitted diseases and even death. However, Castaneda (26 p. 69) (50 p. 36) specifically states that sexual energy is vitally important for *Shamanic Dreaming.*

> … you either make love with your sexual energy or you dream with it. There is no other way.

In order to investigate this claim, we conducted a survey of the scientific literature and found sufficient evidence to implicate the neurotransmitter *dopamine* in an inverse relationship between sex and dreaming. In essence, sexual orgasms release a dopamine antagonist called prolactin (51) and dopamine antagonists are known to suppress dreaming (52). Furthermore, dopamine levels drop below baseline levels after orgasm, and reduced dopamine levels are associated with reduced motivational drive and impaired sustained attention (53). Conversely, dopamine supplementation, such as L-dopa used in patients with Parkinson Disease, have been reported to increase the occurrence of vivid dreams (54) as well as increase sexual libido (55).

In addition, Solms (52) reports that there is empirical evidence that links dreaming with libidinal drive and dopaminergic pathways.

> …there is considerable evidence that dopamine agonists in general (e.g., L-dopa) stimulate excessive dreaming and that dopamine antagonists (e.g., haloperidol) suppress it.

Dopamine plays a key role in reward-motivated behavior, with increases in dopamine levels corresponding to rewards such as food, sex and various addictive drugs [ASAM Definition of Addiction]. Unfortunately, once the rewarding experience is complete, dopamine levels do not return to baseline levels, but often drop below their normal level [ASAM Definition of Addiction].

Various studies (56) (51) (57) have confirmed that dopamine levels rise just prior to orgasm, peak at orgasm and fall thereafter with rising prolactin levels. Prolactin is the hormone that counteracts the effects of dopamine and is thought to provide a sense of satisfaction and gratification. Dopamine levels are theorized to take about two weeks to return to baseline levels after orgasm (57).

It is likely the feelings of satisfaction and gratification, resulting from increased prolactin (a dopamine antagonist), suppress motivation and drive (53). Indeed, when we feel content and satisfied, our motivation and drive are diminished.

Dopamine has also been implicated in various cognitive processes, such as sustained attention, intentional action, behavioral adaptation and anticipatory processes, leading to a conclusion that alterations in dopamine can cause cognitive impairment (53).

Castaneda's assertion that "… you either make love with your sexual energy or you dream with it" appears to be a valid and practical recommendation for shaman neophytes when we consider that; orgasms release dopamine antagonists that suppress dreaming (51) (52), dopamine is thought to play a key role in motivation and drive (53), and dopaminergic dysfunction has long been suspected in the impairment of sustained attention (53). Each of these three components; dreams, motivational drive and sustained attention, is a prerequisite for *Shamanic Dreaming*.

Furthermore, the 'highs' and 'lows' of sex can become a habitual and repetitive cycle of 'pleasure seeking' that keeps the energy needed for *Shamanic Dreaming* always out of reach. Since *Shamanic Dreaming* appears to be a skill that can take years of practice to develop and hone, abstinence for a few days, weeks or even months, does not allow the time necessary to fully develop *Shamanic Dreaming* skills. Therefore, the recommendations by Castaneda and Abelar, for sexual abstinence, seem appropriate for those striving to develop *Shamanic Dreaming* skills.

Another *Shamanic Dreaming* practice (38 p. 244) that reduces reliance on habit and routine is "not-doing". *Not-doings* are essentially actions that engage the practitioner in intentionally breaking habitual patterns and routines by *not doing* what they ordinarily *do*. This technique engages the practitioner in directly reducing attachments to the regular patterns and routines of ordinary daily awareness by becoming aware of their habits and routines, and volitionally choosing an alternate activity.

In support of *not-doing*, as a valid technique for reducing the dominance of habit and routine, Schwartz (36 p. 254) presents empirical evidence that the structure and function of the brain can be reshaped by "... engaging in intentional rather than automatic behavior". Based on this evidence, Schwartz (36 p. 91) developed a technique of redirecting (called Refocusing) attention away from compulsive thought patterns and behaviors – weakening 'entrenched' neural circuits – and thereby reducing dependence on habit and routine. Schwartz's technique is essentially a *not-doing*, since like a *not-doing*, it requires the practitioner to direct attention away from habitual thoughts and behaviors, and toward alternate thoughts and behaviors.

In addition to developing reflective awareness, cultivating volitional control, practicing sexual abstinence and performing not-doings, napping is another dreaming technique that can also free awareness by reducing attachments to the patterns and routines of ordinary daily awareness. Naps are highly recommended as a method to induce lucid dreaming (15 p. 95) (47 p. 151) (58).

Castaneda (59 p. 21) (48 p. 152) (50 pp. 25-26) (60 p. 48) mentions naps multiple times, suggesting that he not only took regular afternoon naps, but used naps to replenish energy and enter dreaming. Indeed, it was during an afternoon nap that Castaneda (2 p. 26) reports he found his hands in dreaming.

But napping is more than a technique to rest the body and induce lucid dreaming, because naps can also reduce attachments to the patterns and routines of daily life by improving creativity and moderating emotional reactivity. Creativity enables seeing the world in new ways, rather than the habitual and routine way of seeing things. And moderated emotional reactivity can provide the pause necessary to recognize habitual behaviors before they automatically take control, and instead make room for alternative behaviors.

Specifically, with regard to improving creativity, Lau (61) found that napping can reorganize and improve relational associations between memories, imparting cognitive flexibility. Additionally, Cai (62) concluded that REM sleep can integrate unassociated information and lead to greater fluidity of thought and creativity. Furthermore, Payne (63) found that overnight sleep and napping restructures memories "so that insights and abstractions can be made".

Napping can also reduce attachments to the patterns and routines of daily life by reducing the impetus of emotional reactions. Gujar (64) and Pace-Schott (65) found that napping improved emotional reactivity to negative emotions and moderated responses to unpleasant events.

Finally, based on research evidence, the Standards of Practice Committee (SPC) of the American Academy of Sleep Medicine (AASM) concluded that Lucid Dreaming Therapy can be considered for treatment of nightmare disorders (66). Evidence indicates that exposure to the fearful condition (source of the nightmare), under safe conditions (such as lucid dreaming), can systematically desensitize the subject to the fearful condition. Furthermore, evidence indicates that nightmares are directly associated with waking anxiety and negative life events. (67) Therefore, *Shamanic Dreaming*, because of its lucidity component, can aid in the treatment and resolution of nightmares and the associated tension, distress and anxiety, consequently freeing perception from the constraints of that fear and anxiety.

Interestingly, in her book *Being-In-Dreaming*, Donner describes an episode with a particularly frightening nightmare (68 pp. 2-3) and her subsequent encounter (68 pp. 19-20) with a seer practiced in *Shamanic Dreaming*. According to Donner, the seer was able to enter into Donner's lucid dreams and provide a remedy for her nightmares.

All the research cited above shows that *Shamanic Dreaming*, and its concomitant practices, can aid the enhancement of volition and the development of reflective behavior - essential elements in overcoming instinct and habit. In addition, practices such as sexual abstinence, not-doing, and napping can improve dream frequency, creativity, intentional behavior, emotional reactivity and cognitive flexibility, thereby reducing attachment to, and reliance on, the patterns and routines that constrain perception to ordinary daily awareness. In essence, *Shamanic Dreaming* practices can help to free awareness from the chains that bind it to the daily world, enabling one to lose sight of the shore and discover new lands.

Activating New Possibilities

The third part of our hypothesis asserts that *Shamanic Dreaming* is a practice that can activate *new possibilities* for perception that that lie beyond the boundaries of ordinary daily awareness. Dreams certainly lie beyond the borders of ordinary daily awareness, and therefore provide an opportunity for perception to experience *new possibilities*. According to Castaneda, *Shamanic Dreams* are, "if not a door, a hatch into other worlds" with the same pragmatic value as the world of everyday.

In reaching for *new possibilities*, shaman found the perception of the left-body (right hemisphere) most useful. Castaneda (1 pp. 139-140) (60 p. 167) tells us that the shaman of ancient Mexico saw that human beings are "composed of two complete functioning bodies", and they used that fundamental division as an opportunity to effectively employ the left body (right hemisphere) in their endeavors to expand awareness.

The idea, that the right hemisphere can present new perceptual possibilities, is supported by neural anatomy within the brain. Specifically, McGilchrist (70 p. 33) offers anatomical evidence that the hemispheres differ in the way in which neurons are predominantly connected, noting that the right hemisphere contains more white matter, indicating the presence of myelination that facilitates rapid signaling across regions. In contrast, the left hemisphere has less myelination since signaling is predominantly within regions. The broad cognitive possibilities, available to the right hemisphere, logically correlate with the numerous myelinated connections spanning diverse regions of the right hemisphere. Likewise, the narrower cognitive view available to the left hemisphere is logically a consequence of neural connections predominantly terminating locally, within the same regions.

An example of the right hemisphere's usefulness, in *activating new possibilities*, can be found in the Aha! experience that accompanies a sudden burst of insight into a problem or situation. Specifically, in an experiment using word-meanings to create insight problems, Bowden (71) found that the right hemisphere employs cognitive processes that particularly facilitate solving insight problems. Bowden points to the theory that the right hemisphere weakly activates distributed neural networks, providing alternate word meanings and more distant word associations, while the left hemisphere strongly activates limited neural networks, yielding a single interpretation and few close associations. In other words, the left hemisphere can become narrowly focused on one possible solution, whereas the right hemisphere can enable a variety of possible solutions. The right hemisphere's *activation of multiple possibilities* enables the Aha! experience to occur when one of the *new possibilities* is consciously recognized as the solution.

As previously discussed, the cognitive characteristics of the right hemisphere provide important contributions to creating new possibilities, including the ability to support broad and open attention, non-verbal imagistic thinking, enhanced creativity, novel associations, divergent thinking, and apprehension of anything new (70).

In addition to those cognitive characteristics, the right hemisphere also has the ability to maintain vigilance at low levels of consciousness. Consequently, when the brain is in a state of low-level consciousness, such as day-dream or sleep onset, the left hemisphere is less active and the cognitive attributes of the right hemisphere are more prominent. Indeed, various studies have shown the advantage of the right hemisphere in regards to vigilance. Cassegrande (72 p. 324) confirms the presence of a neural network within in the right hemisphere that controls vigilance.

More importantly, according to Rotenberg (73 p. 210) the right hemisphere lends ambiguity and more than one possible meaning (polysemantic) to the dream experience, whereas the left hemisphere offers greater certainty and only one possibility (monosemantic).

Evidence suggests that *Shamanic Dreaming*, like lucid dreaming, offers a unique state of consciousness that; 1) largely isolates perception from sensorial data, 2) reduces left hemisphere activation, 3) allows predominance of right hemisphere cognition and 4) enables volitional activity. This unique perceptual condition characterizes the *Shamanic Dreaming* state that Castaneda (25 p. 258) described as "the result of merging my right and left awareness into one in which the order of predominance has been switched and the left has gained supremacy."

Indeed, Cassegrande (74) confirms the possibility that in the absence of sensory input, left hemisphere function may be superseded by right hemisphere function, leading to a "reorganization of cognitive mechanisms".

> Right hemisphere superiority during both drowsiness and sleep states may be useful for the cognitive system when it is operating in a relative absence of external input ...

In addition, Piller (75) and Green (76 p. 159) present compelling evidence to support the position that lucid dreaming involves the right hemisphere in a substantial way, lending creativity, visual-spatial skills, emotionality and non-sequential progression to dreams, at a time when left hemisphere functions are not dominant.

Furthermore, research has shown that ordinary dreams, such as those that occur in REM sleep, show diminished activity in brain regions associated with volition, while lucid dreams more closely resemble waking states, with increased activation in brain regions associated with volition. (77) (43) (44) (46).

Consequently, the state of consciousness that; largely isolates perception from sensorial data, reduces left hemisphere activation, allows predominance of right hemisphere cognition, and enables volitional activity, provides all the perceptual conditions necessary for *Shamanic Dreaming.* Unlike ordinary daily awareness, which constrains perception to the narrow bounds of left hemisphere cognition and grounds it to sensory experience, *Shamanic Dreaming* places perception in a position to intentionally explore and experience possibilities outside the boundaries of ordinary daily awareness.

However, according to Castaneda, *Shamanic Dreaming* seeks to develop dreaming beyond simply achieving dream lucidity, since *Shamanic Dreaming* involves exercises that require the systematic exercise of volition in dreams. In essence, shamanic dreamers are encouraged to progressively develop proficiency in each specific volitional dreaming task, before moving on to the next task. The tasks are grouped into stages, which Castaneda (2 p. 22) refers to as *gates of dreaming*. For example, the first *gate of dreaming* requires the dreamer to volitionally sustain the sight of a dream item, and then learn to move attention from item to item within the dream. The second *gate of dreaming* requires the dreamer to volitionally change dreams, either by dreaming they are having another dream and wake up in the new dream, or by using the items of a dream to trigger another dream. The third *gate of dreaming* requires the dreamer to dream of finding their sleeping body in the ordinary daily world and then to move about in the ordinary daily world. Castaneda (25 p. 261) claims that he was made to "practice every conceivable aspect of volitional movement" during his training in *Shamanic Dreaming*. Therefore, *Shamanic Dreaming* is differentiated from lucid dreaming by the explicit goal of progressively developing and enhancing dream volition.

Furthermore, Castaneda (1 p. 117) reveals that shaman aspire to distinguish between phantasmagorical elements and *energy-generating* elements that appear in dreams. Nearly 3,000 years ago, Homer (78 pp. Book 19, Lines 560-569) poetically expressed this same idea when he wrote about dreams containing elements of both fiction and truth.

> For two are the gates of shadowy dreams, and one is fashioned of horn and one of ivory. Those dreams that pass through the gate of sawn ivory deceive men, bringing words that find no fulfilment. But those that come forth through the gate of polished horn bring true issues to pass, when any mortal sees them.

When sensory input is unavailable, we might expect perception to be filled only with illusory elements - residual products of our mentality, hallucinations, and ruminations. However, some research has shown that perception can be directly affected by energy from the environment, without stimulation of the senses. Therefore, it is possible to become aware of energy even when sensory input is minimal or not available.

For example, bio-magnetic signals generated by the human heart and magnetic stimulation over the temporal lobes are two examples of energy, specifically low level Electro-Magnetic (EM) fields, that can influence perception, without being processed through sensory neurons. In essence, the external energy (EM fields) appears to influence perception by directly affecting neuronal signaling. One theory (79) presumes that the weak magnetic fields "... are less related to direct current induction and more related to field-to-field interactions."

It should be noted that external electromagnetic fields are routinely used in clinical settings. For example, Pulsed Electro-Magnetic Fields (PEMF) have demonstrated significant efficacy in cases of non-unionizing bone fractures. Indeed, a variety of PEMF devices have already been approved by the FDA, to fuse broken bones, heal wounds, treat pain and manage tissue swelling. Clearly, "cells and tissues respond to minute environmental fields of particular frequencies" (80). Additionally, Transcranial Direct Current Stimulation (tDCS) and Repetitive Transcranial Magnetic Stimulation (rTMS) have been used extensively to study and treat various psychiatric, neurological and cognitive ailments and functions (81) (82) (83). These non-invasive brain stimulation techniques typically generate field strengths between 0.2 and 4 Tesla. However, some experiments have been performed using field strengths around five micro-Tesla (5μT), about ten percent of the Earth's field that is normally around 50μT-60μT. The key difference between the low-level rTMS fields and the earth's magnetic field is in the varying modulation of the rTMS fields.

Of particular interest, Persinger (84) (85) and Tinoco (86) have demonstrated that the application of low-level magnetic fields can evoke changes in perception, such as various smells and even a "sensed presence". Notably, Persinger (87) claims the "sensed presence" effect is predominantly a right hemisphere phenomenon, perhaps affirming the shaman's efforts to employ the left body (right hemisphere) in seeking new possibilities for perception.

In addition, McCraty (88 pp. 36, 38) has presented evidence demonstrating not only the presence of bio-magnetic signals generated by the human body, but also the ability of those signals to radiate and affect other living creatures. The low frequency oscillations generated by the heart appear to correlate with emotions and conscious perception. McCraty asserts that others can not only sense these energy fields but also be affected by them.

> ... evidence now supports the perspective that a subtle yet influential electromagnetic or "energetic" communication system operates just below our conscious level of awareness.

Furthermore, recent research appears to indicate that humans can perceive the geomagnetic field, albeit without any notable conscious perception. Researchers found that brainwaves of test subjects correlated to static magnetic fields.

Therefore, it is plausible that in an isolated, but vigilant state of consciousness, perception is in a unique position to experience possibilities outside the boundaries of ordinary daily awareness, including perceiving energy directly, rather than through the traditional five senses. Castaneda (2 p. 29) declares that by becoming aware of "currents of unfamiliar energy" while dreaming, the dreamer opens "a hatch into other realms of perception".

The specific state of consciousness that we have called *Shamanic Dreaming* is one that; largely isolates perception from sensorial data, reduces left hemisphere activation, allows predominance of right hemisphere cognition due to the right hemisphere's superior vigilance, and enables volitional control by activating the frontal lobes. The unique perceptual state that allows right hemisphere cognition to dominate allows imagination, creativity, novel associations and divergent thinking to emerge. But it is the executive functions of the brain that bring volition and a modicum of order and control to the non-ordinary perceptual environment created by right hemisphere dominance. Ordinarily, in waking life, left hemisphere cognition dominates and rigidly molds perception to fit the structures dictated by past experience and the sensory data encountered in daily life. On the other hand, ordinary dreams are dominated by right hemisphere cognition and lack volition, order, control and the guidance of sensory input. *Shamanic Dreaming* is a very special state that engages aspects of both hemispheres in a non-ordinary manner, thereby creating a state that; remains generally unconstrained by sensory data and social structures, enables the creative and polysemantic characteristics of the right hemisphere to surface, and simultaneously facilitates a modicum of order and control by way of volitional activation.

The third part of our hypothesis asserts that *Shamanic Dreaming* is a practice that can activate new possibilities for perception that that lie beyond the boundaries of ordinary daily awareness. In support of our hypothesis, we find that dreams include many of the characteristics of right hemisphere cognition and can enable new possibilities, through; open attention, non-verbal imagistic thinking, enhanced creativity, novel associations, and divergent thinking (see Chapter 2: Left and Right Awareness). In addition, we find that right hemisphere vigilance is superior during drowsiness and sleep states, thereby lending support for "a hierarchical reorganization of cognitive mechanisms ", wherein the right hemisphere can gain superiority as one slips into sleep and dreaming. Furthermore, some research suggests that a right hemisphere predominance continues during dreaming. Moreover, lucidity is coupled with activation of frontal regions associated with volitional control. Consequently, the state of consciousness achieved during *Shamanic Dreaming* provides a perceptual environment that significantly differs from the perceptual environment of ordinary daily life, thereby offering "something more than, and above all something different from, the carefully selected utilitarian material which our narrowed, individual minds regard as a complete … picture of reality." Indeed, the perceptual conditions encountered in *Shamanic Dreaming*, not only enable perception to experience new possibilities, but may also open it to perceiving energy directly, since sensory perceptions, which ordinarily dominate, are greatly diminished.

In this chapter, we have presented evidence that *Shamanic Dreaming*, and its concomitant practices, enhance perception by exercising and developing memory, attention and volition, through the use of journaling, prospective memory training, dream recall, gazing, acting without reward, fostering reflective awareness, practicing dream lucidity and volitional activity. In addition, evidence supports our hypothesis that *Shamanic Dreaming*, and its associated practices, reduce attachments to ordinary daily awareness by using the enhancement of volition and the development of reflective behavior to overcome instinct and habit – the same reflective awareness that enables lucid dreamers to detach from the flow of a dream and realize they are dreaming. The practices of volitional activity, acting without reward, sexual abstinence, not-doing, and napping can improve creativity, intentional behavior, emotional reactivity, adaptability, flexibility and fluidity, thereby reducing attachment to, and reliance on, the patterns and routines of ordinary daily awareness. And finally, we have presented evidence that *Shamanic Dreaming* can enable new possibilities and expand awareness into new arenas because it supports the ongoing development of volition and reflective awareness as well as a reorganization of cognition that allows the emergence of right hemisphere characteristics such as creativity, intuition, non-verbal processing, visual imagery, random processing and holistic thinking in conjunction with left hemisphere cognition that contributes aspects such as linear and rational thinking.

In summary, the evidence presented supports our hypothesis that *Shamanic Dreaming* is one of the practices advocated by Castaneda that can enhance and expand awareness; 1) by improving various cognitive processes associated with perception through training; 2) by reducing attachments to the patterns and routines of *ordinary daily awareness*; and 3) by activating new possibilities for perception that lie beyond the boundaries of *ordinary daily awareness*.

References

1. **Castaneda, Carlos.** *Magical Passes: The Practical Wisdom of the Shamans of Ancient Mexico.* New York, NY, USA : HarperCollins Publishers, Inc., 1998.

2. —. *The Art of Dreaming.* New York, NY, USA : First HarperPerennial / HarperCollins Publishers, 1994.

3. **Hobson, J. A.** *The Dreaming Brain.* New York, NY, USA : Basic Books, 1988.

4. **Kihlstrom J., Schacter D.** *Sleep and Cognition.* Washington DC, USA : APA Press, 1990.

5. *Recalling and Forgetting Dreams: Theta and Alpha Oscillations during Sleep Predict Subsequent Dream Recall.* **Marzano C., et al.** Washington DC, USA : Society for Neuroscience, 2011, The Journal of Neuroscience, Vol. 31(18), pp. 6674–6683.

6. *Techniques for inducing and manipulating lucid dreams.* **Tholey, P.** Thousand Oaks, CA, USA : Sage Publications, 1983, Perceptual and Motor Skills, Vol. 57, pp. 79-90.

7. *Lucid Dreaming as a Learnable Skill: A Case Study.* **LaBerge, S.** Thousand Oaks, CA, USA : Sage Publications, 1980, Perceptual and Motor Skills, Vol. 51(3), pp. 1039-1042.

8. *Efficacy of lucid dream induction for lucid and non-lucid dreamers.* **Zadra, A., and Pihl, R.** Washington DC, USA : American Psychological Association, 1992, Dreaming, Vol. 2(2), pp. 85-97.

9. *Dream Self-Reflectiveness as a Learned Cognitive Skill.* **Purcell, S., et al.** Oxford, England, UK : Oxford University Press, 1986, Sleep, Vol. 9, pp. 423-437.

10. *The Neurobiology of Consciousness: Lucid Dreaming Wakes Up.* **Hobson, A.** Mannheim, Germany : Central Institute of Mental Health, 2009, International Journal of Dream Research, Vol. 2(2), pp. 41-44.

11. *The effects of dream socialization in childhood on dream recall frequency and the attitude towards dreams in adulthood: A retrospective study.* **Bachner, J., et al.** Mannheim, Germany : Central Institute of Mental Health, 2012, International Journal of Dream Research, Vol. 5(1), pp. 102-107.

12. *Personality and Dream Recall Frequency: Still Further Negative Findings.* **Levin, R. et al.** Washington DC, USA : American Psychological Association, 2003, Dreaming, Vol. 13(3).

13. *Personality correlates of dream recall: Who remembers?* **Tonay, V. K.** Washington DC, USA : American Psychological Association, 1993, Dreaming, Vol. 3(1), pp. 1-8.

14. *Absorption, psychological boundaries and attitude towards dreams as correlates of dream recall: two decades of research seen through a meta-analysis.* **Beaulieu-Prévost D., Zadra A.** Regensburg, Germany : European Sleep Research Society, 2007, Journal of Sleep Research, Vol. 16(1), pp. 51-59.

15. **LaBerge S., Rheingold H.** *Exploring the world of lucid dreaming.* New York, NY, USA : Ballantine Publishing, 1990.

16. *Reducing cognitive vulnerability to depression: A preliminary investigation of MEmory Specificity Training (MEST) in inpatients with depressive symptomatology.* **Raes F, et al.** Amsterdam, Netherlands : Elsevier, 2009, Journal of Behavior Therapy and Experimental Psychiatry, Vol. 40, pp. 24-38.

17. *Enhancing Autobiographical Memory Specificity Through Cognitive Training: An Intervention for Depression Translated From Basic Science.* **Doost N., et al.** Thousand Oaks, CA, USA : Sage Publications, 2012, Clinical Psychological Science, Vol. XX(X), pp. 1-9.

18. *Implementation Intentions and Facilitation of Prospective Memory.* **Chasteen A., et al.** Washington DC, USA : American Psychological Society, 2001, Psychological Science, Vol. 12(6), pp. 457-461.

19. *Implementation Intentions : Strong Effects of Simple Plans.* **Gollwitzer, P.** Washington DC, USA : American Psychological Association, 1999, The American Psychologist, Vol. 54(7), pp. 493-503.

20. *Prospective memory: When reminders fail.* **Guynn, M., et al.** Berlin/Heidelberg, Germany : Springer Science+Business Media, 1998, Memory & Cognition, Vol. 26(2), pp. 287-298.

21. *Body Position Affects Access to Memories.* **Dijkstra, K., et al.** Austin, TX, USA : Cognitive Science Society, 2005, Proceedings of the Annual Meeting of the Cognitive Science Society, Vol. 27, p. 2469.

22. *Motor Action and Emotional Memory.* **Casasanto, D., and Dijkstra, K.** Amsterdam, Netherlands : Elsevier, 2010, Cognition, Vol. 115(1), pp. 179-185.

23. *The encoding–retrieval relationship: retrieval as mental simulation.* **Kent, C. and Lamberts, K.** Amsterdam, Netherlands : Elsevier, 2008, Trends in Cognitive Sciences, Vol. 12(3), pp. 92-98.

24. *Environmental context-dependent memory: A review and meta-analysis.* **Smith, S. and Vela, E.** Madison, WI, USA : Psychonomic Society, 2001, Psychonomic Bulletin & Review, Vol. 8(2), pp. 203-220.

25. **Castaneda, Carlos.** *The Eagle's Gift.* New York, NY, USA : Pocket Books / Washinton Square Press / Simon & Schuster, 1981.

26. —. *The Fire from Within.* New York, NY, USA : Simon and Schuster, 1984.

27. **Abelar, Taisha.** *The Sorcerers' Crossing: A Woman's Journey.* New York, NY, USA : Penguin Books USA Inc., 1992.

28. *Intensive Meditation Training Improves Perceptual Discrimination and Sustained Attention.* **MacLean K., et al.** Thousand Oaks, CA, USA : Sage Publications, 2010, Psychological Science, Vol. 21(6), pp. 829-839.

29. *Neural correlates of focused attention and cognitive monitoring in meditation.* **Manna A., et al.** Amsterdam, Netherlands : Elsevier, 2010, Brain Research Bulletin, Vol. 82, pp. 46-56.

30. *Attention regulation and monitoring in meditation.* **Lutz A., et al.** Amsterdam, Netherlands : Elsevier, 2008, Trends in Cognitive Sciences, Vol. 12(4), pp. 163-169.

31. *Neural correlates of attentional expertise in long-term meditation practitioners.* **Brefczynski-Lewis J., et al.** Washington DC, USA : US National Academy of Sciences, 2007, Proceedings of the National Academy of Sciences, Vol. 104(27), pp. 11483–11488.

32. *Mindfulness training modifies subsystems of attention.* **Jha, A., et al.** Berlin, Germany : Springer Science+Business Media, 2007, Cognitive, Affective, & Behavioral Neuroscience, Vol. 7(2), pp. 109-119.

33. *Mindfulness Training Affects Attention—Or Is It Attentional Effort?* **Jensen, C., et al.** Washington, DC, USA : American Psychological Association, 2012, Journal of Experimental Psychology: General, Vol. 141(1), pp. 106-123.

34. **Castaneda, Carlos.** *The Second Ring of Power.* New York, NY, USA : Pocket Books / Washington Square Press / Simon & Schuster, 1977.

35. **James, William.** *The Principles of Psychology Vol 2.* Mineola,NY, USA : Dover Publications Inc., 1950.

36. **Schwartz, Jeffrey M.** *The Mind and the Brain: Neuroplasticity and the Power of Mental Force.* New York,NY, USA : ReganBooks / HarperCollins Publishers Inc., 2003.

37. *Going Beyond Motivation to the Power of Volition.* **Ghoshal S., and Bruch H.** St. Gallen, Switzerland : University of St.Gallen, 2003, MIT Sloan Management Review, Vol. 44(3), pp. 51-57.

38. **Castaneda, Carlos.** *Tales of Power.* New York, NY, USA : Touchstone / Simon & Schuster, 1974.

39. *Psychophysiological Correlates of Lucid Dreaming.* **Holzinger, B. and LaBerge, S.** Washington DC, USA : American Psychological Association, 2006, Dreaming, Vol. 16(2), pp. 88-95.

40. **LaBerge, S.** Lucid dreaming: Psychophysiological studies of consciousness during REM sleep. [book auth.] R., Kihlstrom, J., Schacter D. Bootsen. *Sleep and Cogntiion.* Washington DC, USA : American Psychological Association Press, 1990, pp. 109-126.

41. *Volitional components of consciousness vary across wakefulness, dreaming,and lucid dreaming.* **Dresler, M., et al.** Lausanne, Switzerland : Frontiers Media, 2014, Frontiers in Psychology, Vol. 4(987), pp. 1-7.

42. *The Neurobiology of Consciousness: Lucid Dreaming Wakes Up.* **Hobson, A.** Mannheim, Germany : Central Institute of Mental Health, 2009, International Journal of Dream Research , Vol. 2(2).

43. *Lucid Dreaming: A State of Consciousness with Features of Both Waking and Non-Lucid Dreaming.* **Voss, U., et al.** Oxford, England, UK : Oxford University Press, 2009, Sleep, Vol. 32(9), pp. 1191-1200.

44. *Neural Correlates of Dream Lucidity Obtained from Contrasting Lucid versus Non-Lucid REM Sleep: A Combined EEG/fMRI Case Study.* **Dresler, M. ,et al.** Oxford, England, UK : Oxford University Press, 2012, Sleep, Vol. 35(7), pp. 1017-1020.

45. **LaBerge, S., et al.** Lucid Dreaming Verified by Volitional Communication During REM Sleep. [book auth.] C. Koch, J. Davis J. Braun.

Visual Attention and Cortical Circuits. Cambridge, Massachusetts, USA : MIT Press, 2001, pp. 959-963.

46. *REM sleep and dreaming: towards a theory of protoconsciousness.* **Hobson, J.** London, UK : Nature Publishing Group, 2009, Nature Reviews Neuroscience, Vol. 10, pp. 803-813.

47. **LaBerge, S.** *Lucid Dreaming: The Power of Being Awake & Aware in Your Dreams.* Nwe York City, NY, USA : Ballantine Books, 1985.

48. **Castaneda C.** *Journey to Ixtlan: The Lessons of Don Juan.* New York, NY, USA : Washington Square Press, 1972.

49. **Underhill, E,.** *Practical Mysticism: A Little Book for Normal People and Abba: Mediatation Based on the Lord's Prayer.* New York, NY, USA : Vintage Books / Random House, 2003.

50. **Castaneda, Carlos.** *The Power of Silence: Further Lessons of don Juan.* New York, NY, USA : Washington Square Press / Simon & Schuster Inc., 1987.

51. *Prolactinergic and dopaminergic mechanisms underlying sexual arousal and orgasm in humans.* **Tillmann H., et al.** Berlin/Heidelberg, Germany : Springer, 2005, World Journal of Urology, Vol. 23, pp. 130-138.

52. *Preliminaries for an Integration of Psychoanalysis and Neuroscience.* **Solms M.** Chicago, IL, USA : Chicago Institute for Psychoanalysis, 2000, Annual of Psychoanalysis, Vol. 28, pp. 179-200.

53. *Dopamine and the regulation of cognition and attention.* **Nieoullon, A.** Amsterdam, Netherlands : Elsevier, 2002, Progress in Neurobiology, Vol. 67, pp. 53-83.

54. *Dreaming and REM sleep are controlled by different brain mechanisms.* **Solms, M.** Cambridge, England : Cambridge University Press, 2000, Behavioral and Brain Sciences, Vol. 23, pp. 793-1121.

55. *Dopamine dysregulation syndrome, addiction and behavioral changes in Parkinson's disease.* **Merims, D. and Giladi, N.** Amsterdam, NEtherlands : Elsevier, 2008, Parkinsonism and Related Disorders, Vol. 14, pp. 273-280.

56. *Testosterone Restoration of Copulatory Behavior Correlates with Medial Preoptic Dopamine Release in Castrated Male Rats.* **Putnam S., et al.** Amsterdam, Netherlands : Elsevier, 2001, Hormones and Behavior, Vol. 39, pp. 216-224.

57. **Robinson, M.** *Cupid's Poison Arrow: From Habit to Harmony in Sexual Relationships.* Berkeley,CA, USA : North Atlantic Books, 2009.

58. *Induction of lucid dreams: A systematic review of evidence.* **Stumbrys, T., et al.** Amsterdam, Netherlands : Elsevier, 2012, Consciousness and Cognition, Vol. 21, pp. 1456-1475.

59. **Castaneda, Carlos.** *The Teachings of don Juan: A Yaqui Way of Knowledge - Deluxe 30th Anniversary Edition.* Los Angeles, CA, USA : University of California Press, 1998.

60. —. *The Active Side of Infinity.* New York, NY, USA : HarperCollins Publishers, 1998.

61. *Daytime napping: Effects on human direct associative and relational memory.* **Lau, H., et al.** Amsterdam, Netherlands : Elsevier, 2010, Neurobiology of Learning and Memory, Vol. 93, pp. 554-560.

62. *REM, not incubation, improves creativity by priming associative networks.* **Cai, D., et al.** Washington, D.C. : US National Academy of Sciences, 2009, PNAS, Vol. 106(25), pp. 10130–10134.

63. *The Role of Sleep in False Memory Formation.* **Payne, J., et al.** Amsterdam, Netherlands : Elsevier, 2009, Neurobiol Learn Mem., Vol. 92(3), pp. 327-334.

64. *A Role for REM Sleep in Recalibrating the Sensitivity of the Human Brain to Specific Emotions.* **Gujar, N., et al.** Oxford, England, UK : Oxford University Press, 2011, Cerebral Cortex, Vol. 21, pp. 115-123.

65. *Napping Promotes Inter-Session Habituation to Emotional Stimuli.* **Pace-Schott.** Amsterdam, Netherlands : Elsevier, 2011, Neurobiology of Learning and Memory, Vol. 95(1), pp. 24-36.

66. *Best Practice Guide for the Treatment of Nightmare Disorder in Adults.* **Aurora, R., et al.** Darien, IL, USA : American Academy of Sleep Medicine, 2010, Journal of Clinical Sleep Medicine, Vol. 6(4).

67. *Nightmares, Life Stress, and Anxiety: An Examination of Tension Reduction.* **Roberts, J., et al.** Washington DC, USA : American Psychological Association, 2009, Dreaming, Vol. 19(1), pp. 17-29.

68. **Donner, Florinda.** *Being-In-Dreraming: An Initiation into the the Sorcerer's World.* New York, NY, USA : HarperCollins Publishers, Inc., 1991.

69. **Huxley A.** *The Doors of Percpetion.* New York, NY, USA : Harper & Row, 1954.

70. **McGilchrist, Iain.** *The Master and his Emissary; The Divided Brain and the Making of the Western World.* NewHaven, CT, USA : Yale University Press, 2010.

71. *Aha! Insight experience correlates with solution activation in the right hemisphere.* **Bowden, E., Jung-Beeman, M.** Madison, WI, USA : Psychonomic Society, 2003, Psychonomic Bulletin & Review, Vol. 10(3), pp. 730-737.

72. **Casagrande, M.** Laterality and Sleep. [book auth.] K., Westerhausen, R. Hugdahl. *The Two Halves of the Brain: Information Processing in the Cerebral Hemispheres.* Cambridge, MA, USA : MIT Press, 2010, pp. 313-345.

73. **Pace-Schott, E. , et al.** *Sleep and Dreaming: Scientific Advances and Reconsiderations.* Cambridge, UK : Cambridge University Press, 2003.

74. *Night-time right hemisphere superiority and daytime left hemisphere superiority: A repatterning of laterality across wake–sleep–wake states.* **Casagrande, M., Bertini, M.** Amsterdam, Netherlands : Elsevier, 2008, Biological Psychology, Vol. 77(3), pp. 337-342.

75. *Cerebral specialization during lucid dreaming: A right hemisphere hypothesis.* **Piller, R.** Washington, DC, USA : American Psychological Association, 2009, Dreaming, Vol. 19(4), pp. 273-286.

76. **Green, C., McCreery, C.** *Lucid Dreaming: The paradox of consciousness during sleep.* New York, NY, USA : Routledge, 1994.

77. *The prefrontal cortex in sleep.* **Muzur, A., et al.** Amsterdam, Netherlands : Elsevier, 2002, TRENDS in Cognitive Sciences, Vol. 6(11), pp. 475-481.

78. **Homer.** *The Odyssey.*

79. *The Electromagnetic Induction of Mystical and Altered States within the Laboratory.* **Persinger, M., et al.** Stony Brook, NY, USA : QuantumDream, Inc., 2010, Journal of Consciousness Exploration & Research, Vol. 1(7), pp. 808-830.

80. *Clinical aspects of biological fields: an introduction for health care professionals.* **Oschman, J.** Amsterdam, Netherlands : Elsevier, 2002, Journal of Bodywork and Movement Therapies, Vol. 6(2), pp. 117-125.

81. *Transcranial magnetic stimulation and cognitive neuroscience.* **Walsh, V., Cowey, A.** London, UK : Nature Publishing Group, 2000, Nature Reviews Neuroscience, Vol. 1, pp. 73-79.

82. *Studying and modifying brain function with non-invasive brain stimulation.* **Polania, R. , et al.** London, UK : Nature Publishing Group, 2018, Nature Neuroscience, Vol. 21, pp. 174-187.

83. **Obeso, I., Oliviero, A., Jahanshahi, M., eds.** *Non-invasive Brain Stimulation in Neurology and Psychiatry.* Lausanne, Switzerland : Frontiers Media, 2017.

84. *Experimental Facilitation of the Sensed Presence is Predicted by the Specific Patterns of the Applied Magnetic Fields, Not by Suggestability.* **St Pierre, L., Persinger, M.** London, England : Informa HealthCare, 2006, International Journal of Neuroscience, Vol. 116, pp. 1079-1096.

85. *Experimental Facilitation of the Sensed Presence: Possible Intercalation between the Hemispheres Induced by Complex Magnetic Fields.* **Persinger, M., Healey, F.** Philadelphia, PA, USA : Lippincott Williams & Wilkins, 2002, THE JOURNAL OF NERVOUS AND MENTAL DISEASE, Vol. 190(8).

86. *Magnetic Stimulation of the Temporal Cortex: A Partial "God Helmet" Replication Study.* **Tinoco, C., Ortiz, J.** Stony Brook, NY, USA : QuantumDream, Inc., 2014, Journal of Consciousness Exploration & Research, Vol. 5(3), pp. 234-257.

87. *The Neuropsychiatry of Paranormal Experiences.* **Persinger, M.** Houston, TX, USA : American Neuropsychiatric Association, 2001, Journal of Neuropsychiatry and Clinical Neuroscience, Vol. 13(4).

88. **McCraty, R.** *SCIENCE OF THE HEART: Exploring the Role of the Heart in Human Performance Vol 2.* Boulder Creek, CA : HeartMath Institute, 2015.

CONCLUSION

****

In the introduction, we divided the content of Castaneda's books into three general categories; 1*) the philosophy of the Shamans of ancient Mexico*, 2) *the shamanic practices and methods taught to Castaneda*, and 3) *Castaneda's personal experiences*. We asserted that only the *shamanic practices and their effects* can be probed for scientific validation, since the other two categories are beyond verification. We also declared that the validity of Castaneda's work should depend on the effects of the practices and methods he described, taking into account the full scope of his work.

According to Castaneda and Abelar, the practices and methods they described have the cumulative effect of enhancing perception and expanding the practitioners' awareness beyond normal, traditional boundaries, "to a new area of greater perceptual possibilities". Based on the explanations they provided, the practices are expected to; enhance perception, free perceptual energy, and consequently enable greater perceptual possibilities. Therefore, our hypothesis proposed that the practices enhance perception and expand awareness; 1) by improving various cognitive processes associated with perception through training; 2) by reducing attachments to the patterns and routines of *ordinary daily awareness*; and 3) by activating new possibilities for perception that lie beyond the boundaries of *ordinary daily awareness*.

Throughout this book, we have presented evidence to support our hypothesis for three fundamental practices advocated by Castaneda, specifically, *Magical Passes*, *Recapitulation* and *Shamanic Dreaming*. In each case, the practice was identified with nearly equivalent, well-documented research subjects, since peer-reviewed research on these specific shamanic practices is lacking at this time. However, the parallel between each shamanic practice and its corresponding research topics is justified because of the fundamental similarities. For example, *Magical Passes* possess the same essential characteristics as aerobic exercise, including movements that tense and relax large muscle groups repetitively and breaths to increase the amount of available oxygen. Similarly, *Recapitulation* includes all the necessary components of focused attention meditation, requiring the practitioner to continuously direct and sustain attention on recalled memories, while ignoring distractions. Likewise, *Shamanic Dreaming* qualifies as a type of lucid dreaming since both *Shamanic Dreaming* and lucid dreaming require the dreamer to be aware that they are dreaming and be able to exert some degree of control within the dream.

Based on this equivalence approach, the scientific literature supports our hypothesis and clearly validates the ability of *Magical Passes*, and its modern form Tensegrity, to endow the practitioner with enhanced perception through neurological and cognitive improvements in memory, attention and executive function, primarily due to the aerobic exercise aspect of the movements. Also, numerous studies confirm distinctive characteristics of the *Magical Passes*, such as bi-lateral movements, left body preference, and long sequences of complex movements, that can further promote cognitive benefits beyond simple aerobic exercise. In addition, the relaxation, well-being, and stress reduction benefits of exercise are also well documented. Furthermore, regular aerobic exercise can improve strength, flexibility and balance; benefit the functioning of cardiovascular, metabolic, endocrine, and immune systems; lower mortality rates, and reduce the risk of cardiovascular disease, cancer, diabetes, osteoarthritis and obesity. Therefore, the scientific literature is completely consistent with Castaneda's assertion that *Magical Passes* can endow the practitioner with mental and physical prowess, as well as psychological well-being. Moreover, the neurological enhancements in perception, resulting from the practice of *Magical Passes*, and its modern form Tensegrity, provide foundational support for *Recapitulation*. Specifically, consistent aerobic exercise, like *Magical Passes*, has been shown to improve hippocampal neurogenesis, resulting in improvements in memory and learning. Memory recall and learning (the consolidation of new memories) are the essence of *Recapitulation*.

Research, based on our equivalence approach, also confirms the ability of *Recapitulation* practice to enhance the perceptual process-abilities of memory, attention and executive functions by employing a style of focused attention meditation that utilizes repeated autobiographical memory recall. However, of particular importance is research corroborating the ability of a practice such as *Recapitulation*, to rewrite emotional memories by combining memory reconsolidation (re-learning) and breath, with a calm, safe and relaxing environment. Consequently, *Recapitulation* can revamp the connection between the practitioner's past value-ridden history and present reality ("the remembered present"), effectively freeing psychological and physical energy from memories that bind it to habitual patterns, judgements and behavioral routines, including emotional reactivity. Furthermore, the emotional cleansing of memories, resulting from the practice of *Recapitulation*, directly supports *Shamanic Dreaming*. Specifically, *Recapitulation* practice can diminish the power of emotional memories, preventing them from influencing and clouding perception during dreaming. Moreover, *Recapitulation* provides foundational support for *Shamanic*

Dreaming through the practice and enhancement of visualization, attentional control and memory recall – all fundamental skills necessary for *Shamanic Dreaming.* Indeed, the perceptual abilities associated with forming and sustaining mental imagery, as well as creating active visualizations, are vitally important to support *Shamanic Dreaming.*

In the same manner, a variety of dream research positively indicates that *Shamanic Dreaming*, like lucid dreaming, places the dreamer in a non-ordinary state of perception that largely isolates perception from sensorial data, reduces left hemisphere activation, allows predominance of right hemisphere cognition, and arouses executive areas in the brain to enable volitional activity. In addition, research substantiates characteristics of right hemisphere cognition that support new possibilities for perception by offering "something more than, and above all something different from" *ordinary daily awareness.*

However, according to Castaneda (1 p. 2), shaman were devoutly interested in enhancing perception and breaking the parameters of ordinary reality, not just for the sake of expanding their awareness, but as a means to activate an evolutionary option that allows shaman to retain their individual awareness beyond physical death.

Further clarifying the shaman's goal of retaining their individual awareness after death, Abelar (2 p. 43) emphasizes the shaman's imperative to transform our energy – to complete the "energy body", the "double", or the "dreaming body" – before bodily death, describing the shaman's conclusion that:

> … we die because the possibility that we could be transformed hasn't entered our conception. [Clara] stressed that this transformation must be accomplished during our lifetime, and that to succeed in this task is the only true purpose a human being can have. All other attainments are transient, since death dissolves them into nothingness.

The belief that humans have an *earthly material body* and an *animating energy component*, is common among the major religions of the world. The Bible, the Quran and the Bhagavad Gita share the idea that some part of us, such as a soul, survives beyond physical death. Indeed, it is currently estimated that nearly 80% of the world's population claim affiliation with one of the world's prominent religions (3) affirming belief in some form of existence beyond physical death. Of course, modern science confirms the decomposition of the physical body into "earthly material" after death. However, according to the First Law of Thermodynamics, science also maintains that energy can neither be created or destroyed. Therefore, if sentient beings, such as humans, do indeed possess some, as yet, undiscovered "energy" component – such as awareness, then this portion would continue to exist beyond physical death.

Death is a reoccurring theme throughout many of Castaneda's books, but the philosophical importance of 'Death Is An Adviser' becomes evident when considering the necessity to develop the energy body – to enable awareness to experience the energy at large, beyond the boundaries of the physical body – before bodily death. In this light, it is essential that a shaman confront their mortality and realize the limited amount of time available. Fostering an awareness of one's impending death, can then be viewed as a practical method to motivate devotees into accepting the finite nature of life, assuming responsibility for their mortality, and ultimately spurring them into action.

In summary, this review examined claims made by Castaneda and his associates regarding the practices he advocated, and presented a collection of scientific research and other relevant material which support Castaneda's claims that the practices and methods he prescribed are conducive to enhancing perception and expanding personal awareness. The consequences of enhancing perception and expanding awareness, are beyond the scope of this review. However, Castaneda (4 p. 120) challenges his readers to find out for themselves, claiming that all the tools necessary for personal validation are available.

> [Shaman] gave us the tools. It is up to us individually to use them or refuse them. In essence, we are alone in front of infinity, and the issue of whether or not we are capable of reaching our limits has to be answered personally.

References

1. **Castaneda, Carlos.** *The Active Side of Infinity.* New York, NY, USA : HarperCollins Publishers, 1998.

2. **Abelar, Taisha.** *The Sorcerers' Crossing: A Woman's Journey.* New York, NY, USA : Penguin Books USA Inc., 1992.

3. **Hackett, C. , et al.** *The Changing Global Religious Landscape.* Washington D.C., USA : Pew Research Center, 2017.

4. **Castaneda, Carlos.** *Magical Passes: The Practical Wisdom of the Shamans of Ancient Mexico.* New York, NY, USA : HarperCollins Publishers, Inc., 1998.

www.ingramcontent.com/pod-product-compliance
Lightning Source LLC
Chambersburg PA
CBHW021406090426
42742CB00009B/1025
* 9 7 8 0 5 7 8 4 9 9 1 9 2 *